Household Wisdom

Household
Wisdom

STEPHANIE DONALDSON

TRADITIONAL HOMEMAKING TIPS
FOR MODERN LIVING

COLLINS & BROWN

First published in Great Britain in 2000
by Collins & Brown Limited
London House
Great Eastern Wharf
Parkgate Road
London SW11 4NQ

Published in association with The National Magazine Company Limited.
Country Living is a trade mark of The National Magazine Company Limited.

1 3 5 7 9 8 6 4 2

British Library Cataloguing-in-Publication Data:
A catalogue record for this book is available from the British Library.

ISBN 1 85585 954 8

Conceived, edited and designed by Collins & Brown Limited

Editor: Gillian Haslam
Copy Editor: Emma Callery
Designer: Christine Wood

Reproduction by Classic Scan Ltd, Singapore
Printed and bound by Dai Nippon Printing Co (Hong Kong) Ltd

This book was typeset using Berkeley and Berkeley Book.

Contents

Foreword

by Susy Smith
Editor, Country Living *Magazine*

Welcome to *Household Wisdom*, a book from *Country Living* Magazine on traditional skills that still have a relevance for the homemakers of today. Our homes have always had a great influence on our wellbeing, and at a time when many of us lead fast-paced and stressful lives, it is particularly important to have a calm, ordered environment that provides peace and tranquillity. But we don't want to make additional demands on our time with lengthy housework routines that diminish our enjoyment of being at home.

In the following pages, tips on how to get the most out of labour-saving machines and modern cleaning products are combined with tried and tested, old-fashioned remedies and recipes that are as effective now as they were hundreds of years ago.

Each area of domestic routine is covered comprehensively, with handy shortcuts to achieving instant order and atmosphere in the midst of chaos. This is a book for real people who lead busy lives so the advice given is clear, easy to follow and achievable by everyone. I hope you will enjoy reading it.

Introduction

We live in an age when we are constantly bombarded with images of immaculate homes on television, in colour supplements and advertising; and yet this is also an age when we have less time than ever to do basic housework, let alone the finishing touches that turn a house into a home. In the past, when women stayed at home, much of their daily life was taken up with housework. Labour-saving devices were few and far between, and mothers taught their daughters all the necessary skills before they left to set up their own homes. Today, housework is no longer purely a female affair; we share tasks with our partners (hopefully), we have a machine for every purpose and a product for every task, but we often lack the basic techniques to get housework done quickly and efficiently. Too often we are left feeling inadequate, harassed and resentful in our attempts to live up to our expectations of ourselves as breadwinners, parents and homemakers.

To help with this, this book guides the reader through the home, stopping off in each area to offer advice, tips, traditional recipes and stylists' tricks, which will help keep good order and create pleasant surroundings. The aim of this book is not to create a new generation of 'Stepford Wives' who slavishly read every last word in pursuit of the 'perfect' home, but rather to offer a useful and interesting work of reference, which can be dipped into as the need arises. Scattered through the book are tip boxes with quick tricks to instantly create order and atmosphere in an untidy room. Old-fashioned methods also have a place, but only where they are easy and effective. This is not an exercise in nostalgia – where a modern product is the best solution, this book will recommend it.

Although some of the recommended tasks may involve extra work initially, the resulting order makes tidiness far easier to maintain. For example, an orderly airing cupboard reveals its contents in a trice, while clutter always conceals. However, there is a balance to be struck – hotel rooms are immaculately tidy but who would want to live in one? Cleanliness is important, but tidiness is relative – if you are happy living among clutter then relax and enjoy it.

Think of the most welcoming homes you know – they are seldom the tidiest or the most fashionable. Instead, words like comfort and atmosphere spring to mind – the airing cupboard may be untidy but the bland anonymity of the show house is entirely absent as the owners surround themselves with much-loved objects. Visitors feel free to sit themselves down on the sofa without worrying about untidying carefully arranged cushions, books on the coffee table are there to read rather than as props and the kitchen is the working heart of the home. These people lead real lives and that is what we should all aspire to.

Our homes should be arranged for the pleasure and comfort of those who live within, rather than as a showcase for those we wish to impress. Creativity cannot exist within a sterile environment – an excessively tidy playroom inhibits children's play and bare kitchen work surfaces lead to a reluctance to disturb their order with cookery. If a quick tidy will suffice, you should not feel duty bound to do more. Instead, you will be more relaxed and enjoy your home more when you free yourself of unnecessary chores. This book is not just about cleanliness and tidiness, it's about achieving the quality of life to which you aspire in the place you call home.

THE LIVING ROOM

Carpets and Rugs

The best way to keep your carpets and rugs looking good is to keep dirt away in the first place. When buying a new carpet it is advisable to pay the extra for a treatment that will repel stains and keep the carpet clean for two to three times longer. Dirt-trapping mats at the front door or any external entrance to the room will help greatly and regular vacuuming is essential – it will not wear out your carpet, but trapped dirt will. A vacuum cleaner with a beater bar or rotating brush with variable height adjustment is recommended. To work efficiently it is essential that a bag-type cleaner is emptied frequently or it will be significantly less effective. A new carpet will often shed pile for some time after it has been laid – this is quite normal and will diminish with regular vacuuming.

Cleaning Carpets

Inevitably, spillages and accidents will happen. Instead of carpet shampoos that tend to leave residues which can increase rather than reduce staining, use a solution of a quarter teaspoon of mild, clear liquid detergent to a cup of lukewarm water. First remove any solid or semi-solid substances and then apply the detergent solution to a white cloth or paper towel rather than directly to the carpet. This will prevent saturating the carpet. Starting at the outside and working towards the centre, blot the stain. Repeat the process using just lukewarm water. Spread a cloth or paper towel over the area and apply pressure to absorb as much liquid as possible. Repeat until the stain is removed or it becomes apparent that it will need more drastic treatment. For stubborn stains mix the following two solutions:

◆ 2 tablespoons non-bleaching, non-sudsing ammonia and 1 cup lukewarm water.

◆ 1 cup white vinegar and 2 cups lukewarm water.

Follow the same steps as the detergent solution, first with the ammonia mixture and then the vinegar. Place white paper towels over the area and weigh down with a heavy, colourfast object, such as a washing-up bowl filled with bricks, and leave overnight. Any residue in the carpet should transfer to the towels. For serious stains, carpet manufacturers recommend professional steam cleaning or hot water extraction.

To Remove Dents Left in Carpets by Heavy Furniture

....

Place an ice cube in each dent; and as the cube melts, the fibres will swell. Run over the dents with a vacuum cleaner, which will pull the wet fibres upright again.

Traditional Cleaning of Persian Carpets

....

In the Middle East, rugs would be thoroughly beaten to remove dust, and then laid face down in fresh snow. The snow would draw out the residual dirt and freshen the colours. In Georgian England, a mixture of damp tea leaves and lavender heads was sprinkled over rugs, left to absorb dirt and odours and then brushed off.

CARPETING IN AREAS OF HEAVY WEAR SUCH AS HALLWAYS AND CORRIDORS WILL LAST LONGER WITH RUGS OR RUNNERS LAID ON TOP OF THE CARPET.

Natural Floor Coverings

There is a wide variety of natural floor coverings made as rugs and carpets as well as runners to go up stairs and along narrow hallways. Choose from any of the following but always bear in mind that these floorings are not especially soft under foot.

Rush Matting

Rush matting is a traditional floor covering which, with the correct treatment, can last 25-30 years. A dry atmosphere, particularly that of a centrally-heated house, is its major enemy. To prevent rush matting from disintegrating over time, it should be dampened regularly by misting the entire surface of the matting with a sprayer. In a dry house with wooden floors this can be done weekly, but where there are stone floors or damp conditions, once a month will be sufficient or the underside of the matting may become mouldy. Where possible, roll up the matting twice a year to vacuum the dust from underneath.

Laying Flooring

Natural flooring should be allowed 48 hours to acclimatize in the room before it is trimmed and fitted. It should always be laid by a professional fitter.

Sisal, Jute and Coir Floor Coverings

There was a time, not long ago, when these types of floor covering were considered inferior and not suitable for use in the better rooms of the house. It was rough underfoot, stained easily and stretched most dreadfully. Nowadays, new technology has solved many of the inherent problems and, provided your natural floor covering has been properly laid by an experienced professional, it will not stretch out of shape. Some are supplied ready-treated with a stain inhibitor – if this is not the case, you can extend the life of the floor covering by having it treated when it is laid.

These types of flooring should be vacuumed regularly using a suction vacuum cleaner (not an upright model as the beater-bars can damage the weave). To remove mud or other solids, carefully lift off the excess, leave the residue until it has dried and then brush along the line of the weave using a stiff brush before vacuuming up the debris. For liquid spills, quick action is required using paper towels or other absorbent materials. Work from the outside to the centre of the spill, blotting firmly until all the liquid is removed. Avoid additional wetting of the area and under no circumstances should you use a conventional carpet shampoo. If the stain persists, consult a professional cleaner.

LEFT: Rush matting is equally at home in a contemporary setting or laid on old polished floorboards.

RIGHT: Natural floor coverings are hardwearing alternatives to traditional carpets – ideal for households with children and pets.

Curtains and Blinds

Curtains need washing or professional cleaning less often if dust and cobwebs are removed regularly using the soft-brush attachment of a vacuum cleaner set on low suction. Where the curtains have heavy fringing or other trimming that may be damaged by being sucked into the brush, cover the head of the brush with a piece of net curtain. This will still remove the dust particles, but without harming the trimming. Take particular care with curtains that hang on to the floor. Before vacuuming or brushing the floor, lift the folds of curtain off the floor, shake to remove any concealed objects and then rest the fabric on a chair or other raised object to allow the floor to be properly cleaned. If the floor has been washed, do not replace the curtains until the floor is completely dry.

BELOW LEFT: CURTAINS THAT DRAPE ONTO THE FLOOR CAN COLLECT DUST AND OTHER DEBRIS IN THEIR FOLDS SO THEY NEED TO BE CLEANED REGULARLY.

BELOW RIGHT: NET CURTAINS CAN BE USED TO CONCEAL AN UNATTRACTIVE OUTLOOK OR TO CREATE PRIVACY.

The frequency with which curtains need washing or cleaning depends on the cleanliness of the air. If you live in an area of high air pollution, or have rooms used by smokers or with an open fire, your curtains will need more frequent cleaning, as will kitchen curtains where greasy dust is convected into the atmosphere during cooking. Regular cleaning not only helps the curtains look better, but in better condition the fabric will last longer.

Use common sense when it comes to deciding when to have your curtains cleaned – professional cleaning is expensive and may be unnecessary if the curtains still look clean and in good condition, even after three years or more. It is generally recommended that all but the most basic, unlined curtains are professionally cleaned. Lined and interlined curtains will not respond well to washing as the different fabrics may shrink at different rates, leaving the curtains with unattractive puckering along the seams and hems. Remove all curtain hooks before washing curtains or taking them to the cleaners and replace any damaged hooks when the curtains are re-hung.

Blinds

Roller, ruched, Austrian, Venetian and vertical blinds should all be vacuumed regularly using a soft brush on low suction. Let down decorative ruched blinds to remove the dust that gathers in the folds. Venetian, vertical and roller blinds with wipeable surfaces can be dusted and then wiped over with a clean, damp cloth soaked in a detergent solution. For wooden Venetian blinds, apply a liquid wash suitable for wooden floors with a well-wrung-out cloth.

If a roller blind will not retract properly it needs re-tensioning. Pull the blind half-way down, remove it from its brackets and then hand-roll the blind on to the roller. Replace it on its brackets and check the tension. If there is still not enough tension it may be necessary to rotate the moveable fixing pin, which is at one end of the roller, before replacing it in its bracket.

NET CURTAINS

Grimy net curtains are easily machine-washed and the addition of a proprietary net-curtain whitener will ensure that they are restored to their former bright white condition.

WHERE SUNLIGHT MAY CAUSE DAMAGE TO PRECIOUS FURNITURE, FURNISHINGS OR PAINTINGS, BLINDS SHOULD BE USED INSTEAD OF (OR IN ADDITION TO) CURTAINS.

Antique Textiles

Precious old textiles should be handled as little as possible and are best preserved under glass, away from direct light, or stored in boxes, wrapped or rolled in acid-free tissue paper. Due to their fragility they should only be cleaned by professionals, and even they may recommend that a textile is left uncleaned rather than risk damage.

However, not all old textiles are untouchable heirlooms – fragments of antique cloth can be made into cushion covers or other decorative objects. Modern patchwork quilts sewn from old fabrics are used as bedcovers and tribal textiles serve as hangings and throws. When you acquire antique textiles you should ask if they have been professionally cleaned recently, and if there is any doubt you should have this done.

Direct sunlight will cause serious fading so old fabrics should be protected from it wherever possible. Dust and dirt can literally rot old textiles and will also attract moths. You can keep antique textiles dust-free in the same way as curtains (see page 16) by vacuuming at low suction with a soft brush attachment. For particularly fine fabrics cover the head of the brush with a piece of net curtaining to prevent any loose threads unravelling. Moths like to be left undisturbed, so take down wall hangings and give them a good shake at regular intervals to prevent them setting up home behind the hanging.

Washing Textiles

Washable antique textiles such as patchwork quilts or lace should never be put in the washing machine, even on a delicates programme. This is for two reasons – first the action of the machine is too vigorous, and second the dyes in old fabrics may not be fast. To test for fastness, dampen a piece of white cloth and very gently rub each colour – if any colour comes off on to the cloth you will know that it is not colour-fast. Providing there is no sign of colour-run you can wash the fabric.

ABOVE LEFT: THE SUPERIOR QUALITY OF THE LINEN USED IN THE PAST FOR TEATOWELS AND TABLECLOTHS HAS ENSURED THAT THEY CAN STILL BE FOUND IN GOOD CONDITION IN CHARITY SHOPS OR AT AUCTIONS.

LEFT: OLD FABRICS WITH FADED OR DAMAGED AREAS CAN BE CUT UP AND USED TO MAKE BEAUTIFUL CUSHION COVERS.

OPPOSITE PAGE: MODERN LIFE DOES NOT GENERALLY ENCOMPASS THE USE OF LACE CLOTHS – USE THEM AS ALTERNATIVES TO NET CURTAINS INSTEAD.

Do this by folding the item loosely and laying it flat in a large container (a bath is good for this) filled with cold water and very mild detergent such as good-quality, colourless washing-up liquid. Gently press down on the fabric to loosen the dirt. If the water is very dirty it may be necessary to repeat this, otherwise you can rinse the item several times until you have removed all traces of the detergent. Remove the textile from the water and leave the excess water to drain away. If possible, this type of fabric is best dried flat. Iron on a low heat with a muslin cloth protecting the surface of the textile.

To Stiffen Antique Lace

Washing removes the body from lace leaving it limp. To restore it, dissolve 25 g (1 oz) of gum arabic in 250 ml (½ pint) of boiling water. Leave to cool. Dip the lace into the solution and leave it to dry. Press, using a cool iron through a muslin cloth.

Wooden Furniture and Floors

The simplest piece of furniture, if it has been well cared for, acquires a beautiful patina in its old age. You want to run your hands over its surface to feel its satiny-smoothness as well as admire it. In doing this you are paying homage to all those who have cared for it over the years and reaping the benefit of their diligence. Surprisingly, this doesn't necessarily involve many hours of polishing. Once a piece of furniture has been sealed with polish, it need only be re-applied occasionally. The National Trust in England wax-polishes the furniture in its stately homes only once or twice a year, the rest of the time dusting or buffing suffices. According to the experts, polish does not 'feed' the wood, rather it applies a protective coating that can build up and actually dull the surface if applied too frequently.

The best furniture polish is one with a high proportion of beeswax, both for the finish it gives to the surface and for its smell, and a cream or solid polish is preferable to an aerosol. Before polishing, dust carefully to remove any surface debris, then apply the polish sparingly with a clean, dry cloth, rubbing it on to the furniture with small circular movements. Leave for five minutes and then buff, using a clean, dry duster.

Always use clean, soft dusters on polished wood and be sure that there are no loose threads or raw edges on the cloth, which can catch on veneers or joints and cause damage.

RECIPE FOR A DEEP CLEANING SOLUTION

Applying the following mixture (not for French-polished furniture) can rejuvenate furniture that has a build-up of polish or is just plain dirty. Mix together one part linseed oil, turpentine and vinegar and a quarter part methylated spirits. Shake well before using and apply with a clean, soft cloth. Work in one direction and change the cloth as it becomes soiled.

Treating Scratches

Treat a scratch immediately with a freshly cut brazil nut rubbed over the damaged area – the flesh will fill the scratch and its natural oils will darken the exposed wood.

WHEN YOU POLISH A PIECE OF ANTIQUE WOODEN FURNITURE, YOU ARE JUST ONE OF THE MANY GUARDIANS WHO HAS NURTURED IT THROUGHOUT ITS HISTORY.

Water Marks

Use a soft cloth to gently apply metal polish to a polished surface which has been damaged by a heat or water mark. This will not work where the wood itself has been damaged.

Fading

Fine furniture should not be exposed to direct sunlight as it will fade the colour of the wood. Blinds at the windows allow you to protect the furniture without restricting its positioning

Stripped Pine

Commercial stripping of pine furniture usually involves dipping the entire piece in a tank of caustic solution. This very effectively removes the paint, but it also removes the natural oils from the wood and can leave it looking bleached and dry as well as weakening joints and dissolving glues. Hand stripping is far kinder to the furniture and retains the natural colour; it is worth paying the extra or even stripping the piece yourself to ensure an attractive piece of furniture stays that way. To restore the lustre to dipped pine, remove any polish using the Deep Cleaning Solution (see page 20) and then treat the wood with a mixture of one part raw linseed oil to two parts white spirit applied with a soft, clean cloth. Do this daily until the wood has soaked up all it needs and the mixture sits on the surface. Leave for a few days and then polish with a beeswax polish.

Woodworm

The best way to check for active woodworm is to shine a torch over a piece of furniture. Clean wood inside the holes and on the freshly cut edges indicate live grubs. On polished surfaces you will need to use woodworm killer in a plastic injector bottle applied to the holes at 5-cm (2-in) intervals; unfinished surfaces can be painted with the fluid. If practical, after the treatment wrap the furniture in plastic for a couple of days.

THE SMELL OF POLISH

There is something very reassuring about the smell of polish; it gives the impression of a loved home and cherished furniture. Rather than smothering every surface with far too much of the stuff (see page 20), keep a can of good quality aerosol polish at hand and simply spray it in the air after you have dusted.

ABOVE: HAND-STRIPPED PINE RETAINS THE DEEP, WARM, GOLDEN COLOURING OF THE WOOD WHICH IS FREQUENTLY LOST WHEN PINE IS COMMERCIALLY STRIPPED BY DIPPING IN A TANK OF CAUSTIC SOLUTION.

OPPOSITE PAGE: WOODEN FLOORS AND STAIRS NEED LITTLE MAINTENANCE BEYOND BRUSHING AND AN OCCASIONAL POLISH.

Wooden Floors

There are two types of wooden floor – solid and veneer. The veneer floor is a comparatively modern introduction and usually consists of a thin layer of timber glued to a composite backing. Unlike a real wood floor, it can be laid on to a solid base, which makes it possible to have wooden floors where they would previously have been impractical or prohibitively expensive. This type of flooring is supplied ready-sealed and the only maintenance required is regular brushing with a soft brush (or vacuuming), and washing when dirty with a specially formulated 'wood-wash'. The regular and highly finished appearance of veneer flooring means that it does not age as well as a solid wood floor and particular care should be taken to avoid damaging the surface, as sanding is not always possible.

The care of solid wood floors depends on the finish. Some floors are simply sealed with a matt sealant to preserve the natural appearance of the wood, and the only cleaning they require is simply brushing or vacuuming and wiping over with a damp cloth or mop.

Floors that have been stained to darken their appearance while still allowing the grain to show through, or limed to lighten the wood, usually have a polished finish. This can be brushed or vacuumed and should only need a light application of fresh polish twice a year. Too much polish will cause a build-up and smears, which will show every mark.

Wooden floors may also be painted with a coat of gloss, eggshell, floor or deck paint, in which case the opaque paint completely conceals the natural appearance of the wood. This type of finish is not recommended for high-traffic areas as it will very quickly become scuffed. Clean by brushing or vacuuming and occasionally wiping over with a damp cloth or mop.

FLOOR DUSTING CLOTHS

Impregnated floor dusting cloths will attract dust and give the floors a light shine. To make your own cloths, cut an old woollen blanket into squares and soak them in a mixture of equal quantities of paraffin (kerosene) and malt vinegar. Hang them out to dry and store in airtight plastic bags when not in use.

Metalware

Cleaning and polishing metals with the wrong materials is more harmful than a layer of tarnish. Coarse cloths and abrasive powders can scratch and wear away the surface.

Silver

For regular cleaning of lightly tarnished silver use a long-term silver polish applied and then gently rubbed away with a very soft cloth. Heavily tarnished silver is best cleaned with silver dip, but contrary to its name, you should not dip the pieces of silver into the solution. Dab it on using cotton wool balls, which should be discarded as they become discoloured. Clean a small area at a time and rinse the solution off under cold running water. Once the item is clean, dry it thoroughly with a very soft cloth or even a hairdryer as dampness encourages tarnish.

Silver that has been lacquered does not require polishing. However, the lacquer does yellow with age and when this happens will need professionally removing and reapplying. Do not attempt to do this yourself.

Silver should be stored away from the air. If you want to display it, it is best kept in a glass-fronted cupboard, otherwise it should be

BELOW LEFT: YOU CAN SAVE YOURSELF TIME AND TROUBLE BY HAVING RICHLY DECORATED PIECES OF SILVER PROFESSIONALLY VARNISHED.

BELOW: NEVER BE TEMPTED TO POLISH PEWTER. IT WILL NOT LOOK GOOD AND WILL BE WORTH A FRACTION OF ITS ORIGINAL VALUE.

OPPOSITE PAGE: CUT DOWN ON POLISHING SILVER BY DISPLAYING IT BEHIND GLASS WHEN NOT IN USE. THIS WILL REDUCE TARNISHING.

wrapped in acid-free tissue paper or a soft cloth bag, ideally one of the proprietary bags that has been impregnated to inhibit tarnishing. Chamois leather, felt or baize can all actively cause tarnishing, and never wrap silver in newspaper as newsprint can harm the metal.

Bronze

Bronze should never be cleaned, except for a light dusting. Any other form of cleaning may damage the patina. Dust lodged in cracks and crevices can be removed using a toothpick wrapped with clean, dry cotton wool.

Pewter

Do not polish pewter as the dull, grey patination is an important part of its appeal. Simply dust with a soft cloth or a chamois leather.

Brass and Copper

For lightly tarnished brass and copper use a long-term silver cloth – each metal should have its own cloth, and neither should ever be used on silver.

For heavily tarnished brass and copper use a cream polish. Apply using pads of cotton wool and then polish with a soft, clean cloth. A soft toothbrush or a specialist plate brush can be used to remove polish from cracks and crevices. Kitchen copperware can be given a gleam that will not taint food by rubbing the surface with the cut surface of a lemon.

Professional Secrets Revealed

Around the world, museums, galleries and historic houses use a special wax to protect metalware and other precious objects. Renaissance Wax, lightly applied, forms a protective layer that inhibits tarnishing for a considerable period of time. See pages 122-125 for suppliers.

Pictures

Paintings, prints and photographs help stamp your personality on a room – identically decorated and furnished rooms can look quite different when the pictures are added. One person may choose a single dramatic oil painting as a focal point in the room, while another may choose groups of prints or photographs to create a very different, more intimate and enclosed effect.

No picture should be exposed to direct light and in some cases even a picture light or direct light from a lamp will cause damage and fading. Similarly, damp conditions can cause irreparable damage, as can hanging pictures directly over a radiator.

Watercolours

These are among the most sensitive of pictures, reacting badly to light and to humidity. They should be hung away from direct light and should not be illuminated by a picture light or other artificial light.

'Foxing' or mould is another problem with watercolours and is caused by high humidity. It can be prevented by ensuring that the glass of the frame does not touch the actual picture and that the frame is not hung flat against the wall. A slice of cork stuck to each corner on the back of the frame will allow good air circulation behind the picture. Foxing is unlikely to happen in the dry atmosphere of a modern centrally-heated home. A previously damaged watercolour can be professionally restored.

Oils

When it comes to caring for oil paintings, the general advice is leave well alone. Even dusting can damage an oil as the fibres from the duster may catch on the paint and lift it. Cleaning grimy oil paintings should be left to a professional who will remove the discoloured varnish and apply a new, more stable varnish. If you have an oil painting in an out-of-date or otherwise unsuitable frame, try

ABOVE: A PICTURE DOES NOT ALWAYS REQUIRE A MOUNT AND A FRAME TO LOOK GOOD. SOMETIMES A SIMPLE CLIP FRAME WILL SUFFICE, OR IN THE CASE OF AN OIL PAINTING, NO FRAME AT ALL.

removing the frame altogether – oils often look better without the distraction of a frame, especially in a contemporary setting.

Prints and Drawings

Old prints and drawings should be treated in a similar way to watercolours, keeping them away from direct natural or artificial light, humidity and radiators.

Photographs

Photographs will fade over time if kept on display. One way of ensuring that your treasured pictures of family occasions do not fade from view is to make a habit of ordering two prints and storing one in an archival quality album. Most modern colour photographic prints are inherently unstable – they may look fine for ten years, but forty years on they will be seriously discoloured or faded. Some colour photography papers are more stable and durable than others, so specify this when having film developed or enlargements made if you would like your pictures to last beyond the next generation.

HANGING A GROUP OF PICTURES

When hanging a group of pictures you will find it far easier to mark out a similar area on the floor and play with the positioning of the pictures on the ground before you actually hang them on the wall. You can move them around in relation to one another and adjust the spaces between the pictures without leaving a myriad of little holes in the wall. Use a step ladder to get a proper perspective view of the final arrangement – at this stage it is a good idea to have someone helping make adjustments or you will be continuously running up and down the ladder.

LEFT: SAMPLERS ARE PARTICULARLY VULNERABLE TO DAMAGE BY MOTHS AND OTHER INSECTS AND SHOULD THEREFORE ALWAYS BE FRAMED BEHIND GLASS. IF EXPOSED TO DIRECT SUNLIGHT, THE COLOURS FADE RAPIDLY SO HANG SAMPLERS AWAY FROM STRONG NATURAL OR ARTIFICIAL LIGHT. CLEANING, STRETCHING AND RE-FRAMING SHOULD ALL BE DONE PROFESSIONALLY.

RIGHT: THERE IS AN INFORMAL CHARM WHEN PICTURES ARE GROUPED TOGETHER. INDIVIDUAL PICTURES DO NOT NEED TO BE OF PARTICULAR ARTISTIC MERIT, NOR DO THEY NEED TO BE IN THE SAME MEDIUM OR OF A SIMILAR THEME FOR THE OVERALL EFFECT TO WORK.

Books

If yours is a 'bookish' household there is a strong likelihood that the books are not all stored in ideal conditions: with bookshelves long filled there will be piles of books on all available, and sometimes unavailable, surfaces. Before embarking on building or buying more shelves, a clear-out may be in order. Most of us keep books we will never look at again, which is fine if space permits but not very sensible if it doesn't. Once space has been created you will be able to care properly for the remaining books.

The chances are that the value of the vast majority of books you own will be in the content rather than the book itself, but nonetheless all books deserve to be well looked after. Central heating ensures that the old pests that used to affect books seldom cause trouble these days. If you find an infestation of silverfish it indicates that there is dampness in the area, which should be investigated. Serious damage can occasionally be caused by mice who find books provide ideal nesting material; this is unlikely in a well-used room but can happen in a guest bedroom or other room that is only visited now and then.

Once your books are safely arranged on shelves they will need to be dusted every now and then. In general, this is better done with a small brush attachment on the vacuum cleaner set on low suction instead of a duster, which tends to dislodge the dust to go elsewhere. Once a year, remove the books from their shelves and give the shelves a thorough clean – even the cleanest house will conceal a surprising amount of dust behind the undisturbed rows of books.

HOW TO HANDLE A BOOK

It is amazing how many people do not handle books properly, resulting in a great deal of unnecessary damage. Books should not be removed from shelves by their spines as this inevitably weakens the binding. Ideally, you should lay your hand along the top of the book and curve your fingers over the back and gently pull the book towards you. This works well unless the books are very tightly packed on the shelves, in which case you may have to push down on the top of the book and tilt it towards you. When reading a book always turn the pages by holding the outside edge of the page, not close to the binding as this can tear the paper. Develop the habit of using a bookmark – it's so much better than folding over the corner of a page.

Fireplaces and Stoves

Regularly used chimneys should be swept annually as chimney fires are caused by a build-up of soot. It is false economy to do this less often as anyone who has experienced a chimney fire will confirm. It is a terrifying experience – there is a noise like an express train as the burning soot causes a rapid updraft of air and if uncontrolled it can threaten the whole building. On the sweep's annual visit you should also ask for any chimney that has been out of use to be checked. It may be blocked by a bird's nest or other debris and this will only become apparent when you try to light a fire.

If, in spite of everything, your chimney does catch fire, your first action should always be to call the fire brigade. If, however, there is a delay in them arriving, you can do what the fire brigade will probably do in the first instance, which is to pour teacups of water on to the fire. This creates steam, which will help put out the fire. Don't be tempted to put on larger amounts of water as this will probably douse the fire and no further steam will be produced. If possible, move rugs and furniture away from the fireplace and put a guard around the fire to prevent burning soot falling into the room. Before leaving the room, shut any windows and then close the door as you leave to minimize the draught.

The Grate and Hearth

The grate is the metal basket or other container that confines the fire; the hearth is the floor of the fireplace. The grate lifts the fire above the ground and creates a draught, which helps the fire to burn steadily. Every chimney has its own characteristics and burns differently so there are no hard and fast rules about the best type of grate for a fireplace. Some chimneys draw well, while others do not, resulting in smoke escaping into the room. Sometimes all that is needed is a grate that is lifted well above the hearth, thus improving the air circulation and stopping the smoking. If this does not cure the

ABOVE: A MINIATURE BUCKET MAKES AN ATTRACTIVE AND APPROPRIATE CONTAINER FOR MATCHES. LONG-HANDLED MATCHES WILL HELP TO PREVENT BURNT FINGERS WHEN LIGHTING FIRES.

LEFT: CHIMNEYS OF STOVES AND FIREPLACES MUST BE SWEPT ANNUALLY TO REMOVE SOOT, TAR AND OBSTRUCTIONS, WHICH MIGHT CAUSE CHIMNEY FIRES.

problem it may be necessary to put a baffle plate along the top edge of the opening, or, if all else fails, install an extractor fan in the chimney.

When buying a grate bear in mind the fuel you are planning to burn. For logs you can use a firebasket with well-spaced bars, but if you are going to burn coal you will need a grate that will hold the coal securely and not allow it to drop through the bars as it burns. Grates need no real maintenance and will last indefinitely.

York stone or slate at least 2.5 cm (1 in) thick or fireproof bricks make the best hearths. All these materials can be used under the fire as well as for the area of hearth that extends into the room. Tiles or other heat-sensitive materials must not be used under the fire itself.

Use common sense when clearing out the grate and hearth – even when the remains of a fire appear to be quite cold there can be hot embers embedded in the ash. You will need a fireproof container such as a metal bucket, a small shovel and a dustpan and brush. Use the shovel to gather up all the ashes and put them in the bucket and then brush the grate and hearth. After the dust has settled, the front area of the hearth can be wiped down with a damp floor cloth.

The Fire Surround

Caring for your fire surround depends on the material from which it is made. Painted wood or tiled surrounds only need a regular wipe-

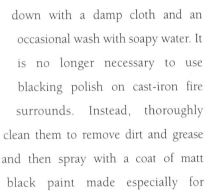

down with a damp cloth and an occasional wash with soapy water. It is no longer necessary to use blacking polish on cast-iron fire surrounds. Instead, thoroughly clean them to remove dirt and grease and then spray with a coat of matt black paint made especially for

fireplaces and wood-burning stoves. Slate should be wiped with a damp cloth to remove dust and given a light sheen by rubbing over with a cloth soaked in linseed oil.

Scratches can be removed by gently rubbing the damage with very fine wet and dry sandpaper. Marble is delicate and is best protected with a microcrystalline wax (see suppliers' list on pages 122-125). This will help protect the surface from smoke and stains. Previous smoke damage can be removed by very gently rubbing the marble with powdered pumice and water – if this does not remove all the staining, rub the area with a half lemon and then quickly wipe clean or the acid in the juice may eat into the stone. If in doubt, or in possession of a fine antique fireplace, call on the services of a professional restorer.

Wood-burning Stoves

Wood-burning stoves are a far more efficient way of heating a room than the conventional open fireplace. With a stove, 30-70% of the heat produced actually warms the room whereas a fire only releases 10-20% of its heat into the room – the rest just disappears up the chimney. A wood-burning stove must only be installed into a chimney with a lined flue – this is an important safety measure and should never be omitted. As the positioning of the stove and its installation must conform to safety requirements it is essential to enlist professional help.

Depending on the type of stove installed you will be able to burn wood or wood and coal. Remove wood ash regularly, leaving a bed of ash 2.5 cm (1 in) thick but coal ash must be removed daily. To prevent a dangerous build-up of resin in the flue when burning wood, it is important to fire-up the stove at least once a day rather than leave it damped down all the time. Flues must be swept a minimum of once a year.

LIGHTING A FIRE

Whether you burn wood or coal, the key to a successful fire is to have the right materials. First you need some highly-flammable tinder to light the fire – firelighters, newspaper or very dry twigs are all suitable. Lay this in the centre of the clean grate, then stack short lengths of dry wood, known as kindling, around the tinder. Light the tinder, and once the kindling has caught fire gradually add the main fuel in the shape of logs or coal. Well-seasoned hardwood logs are best as they burn slowly and give out plenty of heat, whereas softwood logs burn rapidly, give out less heat and their resin will build up inside the chimney, forming creosote which can catch fire if the chimney isn't cleaned regularly. Fruitwood logs burn well and are pleasantly fragrant.

Some fires burn best if the ashes are cleared after every fire, while others work best when a bed of ashes is left in place under the grate. As you become familiar with your fireplace you will find out which works best for you. Wood ash can be spread on the compost heap but the ash from a coal fire cannot.

A WOOD-BURNING STOVE USES ITS FUEL MORE ECONOMICALLY AND HEATS A ROOMS MUCH MORE EFFECTIVELY THAN AN OPEN FIRE.

Potpourris

Today we consider potpourris, pomanders and sweet bags as delightfully fragrant accessories for the home. But they have their origins in the Middle Ages when they were the essential armoury used to protect the home and its inhabitants from the dreadful smells, pests and diseases of everyday life. The preparation of these essentials was an important part of the medieval housewife's duties. In her stillroom, using home-grown aromatic herbs and fragrant petals blended with costly imported spices and fixatives such as ambergris and orris root, she would skilfully blend the ingredients together according to recipes handed on from one generation to the next. The words pot and pourri actually mean 'rotten pot' and refer to the fact that the earliest potpourris were made from fresh rather than dried ingredients, layered with salt, covered and left to cure. This type of potpourri does not look attractive and was traditionally kept in a covered pot with a pierced lid.

The potpourris we make today are not very different from those of the medieval housewife, although they are now a lot easier to concoct. We can avail ourselves of concentrated essential oils, which give the mixture a long-lasting fragrance; dried herbs and flower petals can be bought over the counter, and spices are no longer considered luxury commodities.

A potpourri has four components – essential oils, spices, fixative and a mixture of herbs, flowers, peel and leaves, which give the mixture its bulk. Essential oils vary enormously in price depending on how expensive they are to produce, rose and jasmine being among the most costly. Be cautious about cheap versions – they are either synthetic or diluted. Because pure essential oils are highly concentrated they can cause irritation – good brands will have an

information leaflet giving guidance on the oils that are safe to use. A fixative is one of a number of materials that have the ability to hold the fragrance within the potpourri and prevent it rapidly evaporating. Ambergris and musk are no longer used as they are derived from animals, but orris root powder, gum benzoin, tonquin beans and oak moss can be obtained from herbalists and specialist suppliers.

A home-made potpourri will not have the intrusive and sometimes overwhelming scent that one finds in commercial versions, which are made with artificial fragrances and chemical fixatives that lack the subtlety of natural aromatics. Nor will the fragrance of your potpourri last as long but you can always refresh it by adding a few drops of essential oil or, surprisingly, a tablespoon of brandy.

SUMMER GARDEN POTPOURRI

1 tbsp powdered allspice

1 tbsp coarsely ground cinnamon

1 tbsp coarsely ground cloves

1 tbsp orris root powder (see suppliers' list)

5 drops rose geranium oil

5 drops bergamot oil

3 cups dried rose petals

2 cups lavender flowers

1 cup lemon verbena leaves

1 cup scented geranium leaves

Combine the spices and orris powder in a small bowl. Add the oils, stirring to blend well. Combine the dried ingredients in a large bowl and then add the spice blend, mixing thoroughly until the spices are evenly distributed. Place the potpourri in a large, lidded jar or bowl and leave to cure in a dark place for six weeks. Give the mixture a stir or shake daily.

Pomanders

Like potpourris, the pomander has its origins in the Middle Ages. Originally known as 'pomme d'ambre' it was a small apple-shaped lump of ambergris, which was carried to ward off infection and foul smells. Before long, pierced cases of silver, gold, porcelain and wood were made to hold the ambergris and these became known as pomanders.

The pomanders we know today are an altogether simpler affair consisting of an orange studded with cloves and then left to cure for four weeks in a mixture of spices. Tied with ribbon, it can be hung in a wardrobe or cupboard to add fragrance and repel moths. A properly made pomander will remain fragrant for many years although it will eventually shrink to a fraction of its original size.

A Recipe for Pomanders

Makes 6

100 g (4 oz) ground cinnamon

50 g (2 oz) ground cloves

15 g (½ oz) ground allspice

15 g (½ oz) freshly grated nutmeg

15 g (½ oz) freshly ground coriander seeds

25 g (1 oz) orris root powder (see suppliers' list)

6 oranges without blemishes (Seville are best)

100 g (4 oz) whole cloves

Mix together the spices and the orris root in a bowl large enough to hold all the oranges. Stud each orange with cloves leaving space between the cloves to allow for shrinkage. The cloves can cover the entire orange or be arranged in a pattern. To prevent sore fingers, wear a thimble to press the cloves into the orange or pierce the skin with a toothpick. Roll the completed oranges in the spice mix and then bed them in the spices. Cover the bowl with a lid and stand it in a warm, dry place for four weeks. Turn the pomanders every day. If you notice the spice mix is becoming damp, replace the lid with a cloth until the mixture has dried out. After four weeks the pomanders will be harder, smaller and ready for use.

Quick Ways to Scent a Room

Half-fill a small spray bottle with water and add 20 drops of your favourite essential oil. When you need to freshen a room give the bottle a good shake and then spray into the air – the scent will linger for quite a while. Alternatively, light a candle or two, wait until there is a pool of wax at the base of the flame, blow the candle out and then add one or two drops of essential oil to the melted wax and re-light – the fragrance will gently diffuse into the room. If you have wooden floors you can crush a few lavender heads underfoot to release their evocative scent.

Cut Flowers

When cutting flowers from your own garden, avoid doing so in the heat of the day – the best time is in the morning after the dew has dried, but before the sun becomes too strong. All cut flowers, whether home-grown or shop-bought, will benefit from conditioning before they are arranged. To do this, cut off the ends of the stems and stand the flowers in deep lukewarm water in a cool place for a few hours – or ideally overnight. This will substantially lengthen the flowers' vase-life.

Any flowers that have a tendency to be floppy will benefit from having their stems sealed by submerging the bottom 5 cm (2 in) of the stems in a jug of boiling water. Iceland poppies, ranunculus and hellebores all need this treatment, and many other flowers such as roses, lilac and philadelphus will last far longer if first sealed. Peonies and hydrangeas can be difficult as cut flowers, but respond better if you first fill a bath with lukewarm water and leave them to float in the water for a few hours.

To prevent the stems of tulips and gerberas drooping in the vase bunch the flowers and bind together the stems with twine all the way from the base to just under the flowers. Stand them in deep water for a couple of hours and then arrange – the stems will remain straight.

FLOWER FOOD

Adding flower food to a vase is another way to extend the life of an arrangement as it both feeds the flowers and inhibits the bacteria, which produce slime and smelly water. You can make your own flower food by adding a teaspoon each of sugar, vinegar and non-concentrated bleach to each litre of water.

LEFT: As tempting as it is to arrange freshly cut flowers immediately after picking, they will last longer and look better if they are conditioned beforehand.

RIGHT: Sometimes two smaller arrangements using contrasting flowers in different containers can be more effective than a single large arrangement with everything crammed in together.

FAR RIGHT: Some outdoor plants such as pansies or violas can be used as short-term houseplants in a light but cool position.

Houseplants

There is a world of difference between a healthy, flourishing houseplant and the sad specimens that die a slow, lingering death on the windowsills and mantelpieces of far too many homes. The mortality rate among houseplants is staggeringly high – half the fatalities are killed by kindness such as over-watering and over-feeding, while the other half starve to death – an occasional splash of water and no feed.

It is not difficult to grow houseplants successfully provided that you first select plants that are suitable for your home environment. Direct sunlight and a dry atmosphere may be heaven for pelargoniums but they are hell for ferns, while no plant will last long in a windowless bathroom. Before you buy, look at the labels and be guided by the symbols, which will help you choose the right plant for your conditions.

It is not always appreciated that commercial potting composts contain a limited supply of plant food – usually sufficient for about six weeks. So once that initial period is over it is essential to feed the plants regularly to keep them growing during their active season. An organic liquid feed is preferable as the chemical feeds will eventually cause a detrimental build-up of salts in the compost.

With the obvious exception of cacti, most plants benefit from a humid atmosphere. You can help provide this by grouping plants together or standing the pots on gravel-filled saucers, which will retain moisture and keep the roots moist.

Most houseplants will benefit from a spell outdoors during the summer. Stand them in partial shade or they may be scorched by the sun. Their leaves will be washed clean in the summer rain and they will put on lots of new growth.

THE
BEDROOM
AND
BATHROOM

The Bed

Considering that we spend approximately one third of our lives in bed, it is amazing how many of us sleep on uncomfortable or unsuitable beds. There was a time when it was generally thought that the harder a bed, the better it was for our backs, and so-called 'orthopaedic' beds were promoted as the solution to all back problems. This has been disproved and any reputable bed supplier will tell you that the best bed is the one that you find most comfortable and supportive – neither too hard nor too soft.

Where a bed has its own base, it is important to replace the base along with the mattress as placing a new mattress on an old base reduces the comfort and life of a mattress. Don't be tempted to buy a second-hand mattress either, however good the condition may appear – it will have absorbed up to a pint of the previous occupant's sweat per night!

Caring for Your Bed

You can ensure that your bed remains in good condition for as long as possible by looking after it properly. Turn the mattress once a month to prevent hollows forming in your habitual sleeping position, and once every three months turn it top-to-bottom as well. Regularly use the soft brush attachment of your vacuum cleaner on the mattress to pick up dust mites and skin scales, which we shed at the rate of 500 g (1 lb) a year. A quilted mattress cover is recommended.

CHOOSING A MATTRESS

The only way to select a mattress is to try it out – good retailers will encourage you to take off outer clothing and lie down. Take a few minutes, or more; after all you are going to spend a lot of time in the bed of your choice. Lie on your back and slide your hand under the small of your back – if the hollow is empty of mattress, the bed is probably too hard; if there is no space for your hand, the bed may be too soft.

If you share a bed with a partner you may find that the same mattress doesn't suit you both, in which case you should consider a bed with separate bases and mattresses, which can be linked together to meet both your needs. Buy the best you can afford – you will be amply repaid with nights of restful sleep.

Choice and Care of Bedding

Nowadays most of us choose to sleep under duvets, although there are a few people who still prefer the heavier and more traditional blankets and quilts.

Duvets and pillows are available in a large range of qualities and fillings. It is generally agreed that the finest duvets and pillows are those filled with pure goose down which, although very expensive, is wonderfully luxurious – a goose down pillow has the perfect balance of softness and support and a goose down quilt is very light yet warm. Other natural fillings consist of a blend of feathers and down, or just feathers; while man-made fillings are preferable for

BLANKETS

The finest blankets, like the best duvets, are made from the most expensive materials – the costliest blankets are very light, very soft and very warm. As a general rule, the coarser the wool and heavier the blanket, the less warm it will be.

anyone who suffers from hay-fever or similar allergies. Synthetic materials tend to be hotter to sleep under because they do not breathe in the same way as the natural fillings. If this is a problem, try using a top-sheet under the duvet.

All bedding should be aired daily. As tempting as it is to plump the pillows and pull up the covers the minute you get out of bed this isn't good for the mattress, the bedding or yourself. Bearing in mind the pint of sweat given off by an individual each night, the bed and bedding need a chance to dry out before the bed is made. In addition to the daily airing, it is advisable to air duvets and pillows outdoors from time to time. Remove all the covers, give each item a thorough shake and leave them in the sunshine for a couple of hours. In the absence of a garden, do as they do in Europe and hang your bedding out of the window. Bedding that is used regularly should be professionally cleaned once a year – blankets can be dry-cleaned and there are specialist companies that will clean down/feather-filled duvets and pillows and renovate covers or fillings when necessary. All bedding with synthetic fillings is washable.

In the event of accidental spills on pillows or duvets with natural fillings, where the spill is localized shake the filling away from the spillage and sponge the area clean. Where pillows are badly affected they can be individually machine-washed and tumble-dried – a seemingly ruined pillow can be rescued in this way, but this should only be done where the covering is intact and of good quality or you could risk blocking the machine with feathers or down.

OPPOSITE PAGE: WHERE BLANKETS ARE PREFERRED TO DUVETS, USE OLD-FASHIONED QUILTS OR EIDERDOWNS FOR ADDED WINTER WARMTH.

BELOW: AN INFORMAL FOUR-POSTER BED WITH CHECKED BED CURTAINS IS INVITING, COSY AND ROMANTIC. THE USE OF A DUVET AND THROW SIMPLIFIES BED-MAKING.

Clothes

Taking good care of clothes can considerably extend their life, ensuring that the money you invest in your wardrobe is amply repaid. Caring for clothes is not simply a matter of making sure that they are clean and well-pressed – it's also about storing them properly, using the right coat hangers and editing the contents of your wardrobe regularly to prevent over-crowding, which can leave the best clothes looking crushed and forlorn.

Unless you are naturally orderly and a disciplined person, you will probably find that your clothes are in need of a good sort out. Avoid doing this when you are in a sentimental frame of mind, you will get nowhere if every aged relic you unearth has you day-dreaming about the happy times you shared. That being said, you don't necessarily have to get rid of these clothes, but given that they don't fit, are seriously out of fashion, or there is any other reason that they are unwearable, they are better packed away instead of cluttering up your precious storage space. After this initial edit of your wardrobe you can free up still more space by removing clothes that are out of season. These can be stored in a separate wardrobe/chest of drawers or be folded and packed away until the change of season. The added benefit of separating your clothes in this way is that you may have forgotten all about them by the time you unpack them the following season – it's like a whole new wardrobe!

At this point you should find that your storage space has dramatically increased and you can create order where there was chaos. The next step is to get rid of any wire coat hangers and replace them with something more substantial. Jackets, for example, should be hung on properly shaped or padded hangers to prevent the shoulders losing their shape. Finally, the clothes can be sorted into shirts, skirts, suits, dresses, etc. so that you can see at a glance what you have in each category. With a tidy wardrobe you can easily assess what you do or don't need next time you go clothes shopping.

Clothes Moths

Moths are more likely to damage clothes that have been put away dirty, so be sure to wash or dry-clean clothes before storing them. In the days when dry-cleaning was non-existent and clothes were not washed as regularly as they are today, this pest was a far greater problem. Today, rather than using mothballs, which are unpleasantly smelly and not at all environmentally friendly, you should check stored clothes regularly for any signs of moth damage. It is actually the caterpillar rather than the moth that does the damage. Look for small 5-8 mm (¼ in) caterpillars, or their cases, tiny white eggs attached to fibres, or greyish moths flying out of stored clothing. If you do have an infestation, wash or dry-clean the clothes to remove any moths or eggs you may have missed and vacuum clean the affected drawers or cupboards. It is worth investing in some cedar wood balls and coat hangers as they are gentle but effective moth and insect repellents, or you could fill sachets with the pleasantly fragrant moth-repellent mixture given on the right.

MOTH-REPELLENT SACHETS
....

25 g (1 oz) each of caraway seeds, cloves, mace,
nutmeg and cinnamon
25 g (1 oz) tonquin beans (see suppliers' list)
150 g (6 oz) orris root powder (see suppliers' list)

Grind together the spices and tonquin beans (an electric coffee grinder is ideal) and mix in the orris root powder. Fill sachets with the mixture and slip them among your clothes to keep moths at bay. Use a double layer of close woven fabric for the sachets or the powder may escape through the weave.

FAR LEFT: THROW AWAY WIRE COAT HANGERS AND INVEST IN GOOD QUALITY WOODEN OR PADDED HANGERS TO MAINTAIN THE SHAPE OF JACKETS AND COATS.

LEFT: RID CLOTHES OF TOBACCO OR FOOD ODOURS BY HANGING THEM OUTDOORS FOR AN HOUR OR SO.

Shoes

There is an old adage that you can judge a person by the shoes they wear, in which case many of us must be found to be sorely wanting. The most expensive shoes soon lose their appeal if they are unpolished and down-at-heel while a well-cared-for pair of good quality shoes can literally last a lifetime. If you have a favourite pair of shoes that you wear more than any others it makes sense to buy two identical pairs, which you alternate wearing. In this way, both pairs will last far longer and you will not be tempted to delay repairs as you might with only one pair available.

Like beds, shoes need airing after they have been worn – leave them out overnight before you clean them, after which you can insert shoe trees if you wish and then put them away.

Space permitting, one of the best ways to store shoes is in their original cardboard boxes with a brief description written at one end, e.g. flat black pumps, brown suede loafers. Storing shoes in this way ensures they stay dust free and protected. One of the worst ways to store shoes is in a muddled heap at the bottom of the wardrobe!

WELL-MADE SHOES WILL REPAY CAREFUL MAINTENANCE WITH MANY YEARS OF WEAR. UNKEMPT SHOES, HOWEVER EXPENSIVE, CAN SPOIL AN OTHERWISE IMMACULATE OUTFIT.

Perfumes and Other Fragrances

Pretty cut-glass or crystal bottles of perfume may look lovely on a dressing table, but this is not the way to keep your perfume in good condition because both direct light and warmth cause perfumes to deteriorate. To ensure that the fragrance remains stable it should be kept in its box, preferably in a drawer or somewhere cool – the fridge is ideal during the summer.

Perfumes are available in three formulations – eau de parfum is 20% essential oil to 80% alcohol, eau de toilette is 5% oil to 95% alcohol and eau de cologne is 3% oil to 97% alcohol. From this it is clear why eau de parfum is so much more expensive than the other two and why you need only use it very sparingly. Apply it by lightly dabbing it on the pulse points behind each ear and behind the knees. A single application should last all day. Estée Lauder's personal advice on the best way to apply eau de toilette or eau de cologne from a spray bottle is worth following: spray the air above your head and then turn around slowly – the fragrance will drift down and settle all over your body.

The Scented Boudoir

The bedroom is a private retreat, a place for relaxation and intimacy and as such it should be treated as somewhere special, not just a room where you sleep and store clothing. It should be warm and comfortable, but also inviting, and the subtle use of fragrance is an important element in creating the right atmosphere. Scented candles will fill the air with fragrance and give a soft, romantic light, or oil burners can be used to gently diffuse aromatic oils into the air. It is important to choose fragrances that are not too heady or you may find that they overwhelm you and may even leave you feeling nauseous and headachy. Citrus oils such as grapefruit, bergamot and lime are ideal, as is lavender.

TO CLEAR YOUR NOSE OF PERFUME

When trying out new perfumes you can clear your nose by sniffing the sleeve of a woollen coat or jumper.

With all fragrances, whether for the body or for the environment, the most successful result is made up of subtle layers of fragrance rather than a single powerful source. Choose a fragrance you like and apply in layers, such as soap or bath oil, body lotion and a spray of perfume, or use it for scented drawer liners, in sachets slipped among your linen, as a burning oil or scented candles and you will find that the fragrance will gently permeate the entire room, creating the perfect atmosphere for romance and relaxation.

THE DANGERS OF PERFUME IN THE SUN

Perfume should never be applied before sunbathing as it can cause Berloque dermatitis, a rash that causes unsightly skin discoloration.

AS ATTRACTIVE AS OLD SCENT BOTTLES MAY BE, THEIR CONTENTS WILL HAVE LONG CEASED TO SMELL ALLURING. ALL PERFUMES HAVE A LIMITED SHELF LIFE, ESPECIALLY WHEN EXPOSED TO LIGHT.

Creams, Lotions and Cosmetics

Like perfumes, all cosmetics should be stored in conditions that help them to remain stable or they will deteriorate. They should be kept out of direct light and in a cool place.

With the wealth of new products that constantly flood the market, it is inevitable that most of us will have quantities of creams, lotions and cosmetics tucked away in cupboards which we have tried and then abandoned for some reason or other – face creams that proved to be too heavy, too light, too oil;, the wrong colour of tinted foundation creams; lipstick that failed to deliver the promised glamour. There is no point in holding on to these – if you haven't used them yet, you won't, although some can be used for other purposes. Over-rich face creams can become a luxurious treatment for elbows and heels, light moisturisers can be used on the body as well as the face, and teenage girls will be grateful recipients of any cosmetic you choose to pass their way.

It has been said many times that there is no scientific basis for the sometimes dramatic claims that most cosmetic manufacturers make, yet we continue to be seduced by the glamorous images, life-changing promises and glossy packaging. In reality, we could care for our skin just as well with inexpensive, home-made products.

The recipes that follow for a cleanser, toner and cold cream all use pure and simple ingredients, which will not work instant miracles, but will cleanse, tone and moisturize your skin gently, pleasantly and effectively.

ROSE WATER AND ALMOND CLEANSER

Makes approximately 250 ml (8 fl oz)

25 g (1 oz) white beeswax

150 ml (5 fl oz) almond oil

4 tbsp rose water

¼ tsp borax

2 drops rose essential oil (optional)

Place the beeswax in a heatproof bowl and rest the bowl over a pan of simmering water until the beeswax is melted. Whisk in the almond oil. Measure the rose water and borax into another small saucepan and warm gently until the borax has dissolved. Very slowly add the rose water to the melted beeswax and almond oil, whisking all the time. The mixture will emulsify rapidly and as you continue whisking it will take on a smooth, creamy texture. Add the essential oil if desired. Pour the cleanser into a dry glass or china jar with fitted lid and leave to cool before replacing the lid securely.

To use the cleanser, tip a small amount into the palm of your hand and apply to the face with a circular motion using the tips of the fingers. Remove using damp cotton wool. *Note*: Borax is mildly antiseptic and soothing, but should not be used on broken skin.

TRADITIONAL SKIN TONER

120 ml (4 fl oz) witch hazel

50 ml (2 fl oz) rose water

Measure the ingredients into a clean, dry glass bottle and shake vigorously.

To use the skin toner, apply to damp cotton wool and use to freshen skin after cleansing. Skin toner should only be used by those with oily or combination skins. It is too drying for other skin types.

SCENTED COLD CREAM

This cold cream can be made without the scented essential oils, but they do impart a lovely fragrance, and both rose and frankincense oils are very good for the skin.

50 g (2 oz) white beeswax
120 ml (4 fl oz) almond oil
50 ml (2 fl oz) rose water
½ tsp borax
120 ml (4 fl oz) warm purified or bottled water
2 drops rose essential oil (optional)
2 drops frankincense essential oil (optional)

Gently heat the beeswax in a bowl over a pan of simmering water until it has melted. Remove from the heat and slowly whisk in the almond oil. Warm the rose water in another pan and stir in the borax until it has dissolved; then add the purified or bottled water. Very slowly pour the warm water into the oil mixture, whisking all the time. The mixture will quickly turn thick and creamy. Continue to whisk as the mixture cools to ensure an even consistency. Add the essential oils if required. Spoon the cold cream into a clean and dry wide-mouthed container. Leave to cool and then cover.

To use the scented cold cream, gently smooth into previously cleansed and toned skin. It will be absorbed quickly and leave the skin feeling soft and smooth. As this cream contains borax it should not be used on broken skin.

Hair Care

Hair products are big business. One only has to visit the supermarket and look at the bewildering range of shampoos, conditioners, combined shampoos and conditioners, special treatments, gels, waxes and hairsprays to realize that there is much more going on here than selling products to get your hair clean. They are selling a dream – perfect hair, thick, glossy and immaculately groomed. Undoubtedly, some do have a visible effect on the hair, the inclusion of silicon in conditioners does give the hair added shine, and anyone with fine hair, lacking in body, blesses the day someone came up with hair-thickening lotion. However, long-term use of any single product will result in a build-up on hair and scalp, which can totally reverse the benefit. Hairdressers now recommend that hair products are alternated regularly and that they include a shampoo formulated to remove build-up. Alternatively, you can make an old-fashioned hair rinse, which will leave the hair shiny and squeaky clean.

Caring for Brushes and Combs

Hair brushes and combs should be washed once a week. They may look clean, but the natural oils from the hair and residues from shampoos and other hair products build up on them as well as on the hair. Wash them in warm water to which a mild detergent has been added and then rinse.

Real bristle brushes, where the body of the brush is made from wood, silver, horn, etc., should be cleaned by dipping the bristles into the detergent mixture, keeping the back and handle of the brush dry. Rinse in the same way and then dry the brush by standing it, bristles downwards, on a soft towel in a warm place. Antique horn and tortoiseshell combs should be wiped clean with a damp cloth rather than soaked and then wiped over with a cloth dipped into almond oil. This will prevent the comb drying out and splitting.

VINEGAR HAIR RINSE

25 g (1 oz) dried camomile flowers (for fair hair)
2 drops camomile essential oil

or

25 g (1 oz) fresh rosemary (for dark hair)
2 drops rosemary essential oil (do not use rosemary oil
if you are pregnant)

450 ml (¾ pint) bottled water
25 ml (1 fl oz) cider vinegar

Place the camomile flowers or rosemary in a jug. Bring the water to the boil and pour over the herbs. Cover with a cloth and leave to infuse overnight. The following day strain the infusion and add the cider vinegar and essential oil. Use immediately as the final rinse after shampooing or decant into a sealed jar or bottle and store in the fridge for up to one week.

Bath Products

Relaxing in the bath is one of life's simple, but great pleasures. There is nothing quite like it at the end of a stressful day at work; in preparation for a romantic evening; to ease aching muscles after gardening or just as an opportunity for some personal indulgence. You may well have a bathroom cupboard crammed with delicious bath oils and unguents which are lavished upon you at birthdays and Christmas, in which case you probably need little encouragement to linger in the bathroom. But if this is not the case, there are many simple things you can do to transform a bath full of water into a hedonistic experience.

Bath Infusions

These are simplicity itself. Pick a bunch of your favourite fragrant herbs, such as lavender, rosemary, scented geranium and lemon verbena, and tie them together with string or raffia, leaving a loop to hang over the hot tap. When you are running the bath the hot water will draw out the essential oils and make the bath deliciously fragrant.

You can also use teabags for an instant herbal bath. Camomile is softening and calming; peppermint is good for dull, blotchy skin; lime blossom is a deep cleanser and very soothing, while mineral-rich nettles will help cleanse and nourish your skin. Put at least four teabags into a basin, pour over boiling water, cover and leave to infuse for 15 minutes before adding to your bath.

Bath Soaks

Herbal Vinegar: Cider vinegar is a wonderful skin softener; you can combine skin care and medicine by macerating a handful of herbs from your garden in half a bottle of cider vinegar to produce a strong cider vinegar. Leave for a week before straining out the herbs and decanting the vinegar into a pretty bottle. Add a couple of tablespoons full to your bath. Use rosemary for a stimulating morning bath, mint to refresh you when you are weary, thyme or sage when a cold threatens, marjoram as a sedative before bedtime and lavender to ease tired muscles.

Oatmeal and Almond Soak: Mix together a cupful each of fine oatmeal and ground almonds. Place the mixture in the middle of a square of cotton, bring the corners together and tie securely. Hang the bundle over the hot tap so that the water runs through it into your bath. The water will turn milky and feel very, very soft.

Ginger Bath: A ginger bath is warming and comforting for stiff or rheumatic joints. Slice 5 cm (2 in) of unpeeled fresh ginger root into 1 litre (2 pints) of water. Bring the water to the boil and simmer for half an hour. Strain and add to a warm bedtime bath. Wrap up warmly when you get out of the water and gently exercise stiff joints for a few minutes before climbing into bed.

Bath Oils

Your favourite essential oils can be added to the bath for therapeutic purposes or pure pleasure. The oils should be added after the bath has been run, and where the oils are undiluted, you will only need three drops. These are very concentrated substances and adding too much can be unpleasant or even harmful. Camomile, lavender, clary sage, geranium, citrus oils, sweet marjoram, rose, sandalwood, vetiver and ylang ylang are all recommended unless you are pregnant or have an existing medical condition, in which case essential oils are best avoided. Citrus oils have a short shelf life and many are phototoxic, which means that they should not be used before exposure to sunlight or they can cause alterations in pigmentation.

Bathroom Cleaning

A less-than-clean bathroom is not very inviting. Who wants to linger in a bath with a ring around it, or dry themselves on damp pre-used towels, or step over someone else's dirty clothes? Ideally, responsibility for a clean bathroom should rest with all who use it, but as cleanliness and tidiness thresholds can vary enormously this may prove difficult to enforce. Go for the basics, and accept that you may have to do the rest.

Everyone can clean the bath after use. Fill a spray bottle with dilute bubble bath and show young children how they can clean it while the water runs away – they will see it as a game rather than a chore and the bubble bath will do them no harm. Encourage all members of the household to hang up their towel after use – individual towel rails or pegs and different colour towels will help with this. Accept no excuses when it comes to flushing the loo. If space permits, have a large open-topped laundry basket in the bathroom – there is a reasonable chance that some of the dirty clothes will end up in it and it is the work of seconds to throw the remainder in there.

The best time to clean the bathroom is just before you have a shower or bath yourself – obviously not just before a special occasion or when you want to soak away your troubles. Instead, choose a more mundane time when you can allocate 10 minutes to the task. There are two reasons why this is the best time – first, you get to enjoy the freshly cleaned bathroom before anyone else, and second, you can get wet and messy in the process because you will soon be fresh and clean.

The easiest way to clean the shower is when you are showering. Have a spray bottle filled with vinegar and a small squeegee to clean the tiles and the glass screens and prevent the build-up of limescale. The shower tray can be cleaned with a proprietary cleaner as you leave the cubicle, working your way towards the door.

DINGY GROUTING

A bathroom may be spotlessly clean, but if the grouting around the tiles is discoloured it will spoil the effect. Clean the grouting by spraying it with a cleaner containing bleach, and then use a nail brush or washing-up brush to remove the discoloration.

First-aid Kit

Everyone should have a properly stocked first-aid kit in their home and some basic knowledge of how to treat minor problems and, in more serious situations, how to look after someone until professional help arrives.

A first-aid kit should contain a good selection of waterproof and fabric plasters; sterile gauze and cotton wool; crepe bandages; tubular gauze for finger injuries; antiseptic cream; antihistamine cream or a similar product for treating insect bites and stings; a pair of tweezers; a pair of scissors, safety pins and a sling. A selection of painkillers should also be included. The kit should be stored in an easily accessible place, but out of the reach of young children. Check the kit from time to time to make sure that creams and lotions have not gone past their 'use-by' date.

Homeopathic first-aid kits are available with the usual range of bandages and general equipment, but these will also include items such as Rescue Remedy or Arnica 30 to treat shock or trauma, calendula cream for soothing cuts and sores, and pyrethrum spray for bites and stings.

LIFE-SAVING ACTION

Both the Red Cross and St John's Ambulance run short first aid courses, which teach basic, but vital techniques. Attending one of these may mean that you are in a position to save someone's life one day. The chances are that in an emergency situation you will have neither the time nor opportunity to consult a book and the techniques are far easier to remember and use correctly if you have had practical experience in controlled conditions.

Burns

All burns, whether wet or dry, must be treated by cooling. Never apply creams, butter or lotion. The injured area should, if at all possible, be immersed in cold water or placed under a running tap for at least 10 minutes, and in most cases, the longer you can leave the burn in water the better. Once the area has been thoroughly cooled it should be covered by a sterile dressing, or where a large area is affected, with a clean sheet or pillowcase. With any serious burn, medical help should be summoned immediately.

Wounds

Superficial cuts and scrapes can be treated at home, but there are certain indications that a wound is more serious and needs professional attention:

◆ Deep puncture wounds caused by dirty or rusty objects carry a high risk of infection and need medical treatment.

◆ A wound that is pulsing blood indicates that an artery may have been severed. Summon medical help immediately and then cover the wound with a wad of clean cotton and press very firmly for at least 15 minutes to slow the bleeding. If the wound is to a limb, raise it above the level of the heart as this will also slow bleeding.

◆ A jagged wound or one where the cut gapes open indicates that stitches are necessary.

◆ An animal bite.

Natural Remedies

Long before modern medicine came along, people with no access to doctors or medicines were treating themselves with natural remedies gathered from the countryside around them. For many years we were quite dismissive of this type of treatment but we are increasingly turning back to the old-fashioned remedies as we find that modern drugs are not always the universal panacea we hoped for. Furthermore, scientific research reveals that the healing powers attributed to many common plants are not folklore but fact.

Naturally, you should never attempt to treat a serious medical condition yourself. Most doctors are far more open to complementary medicine today and you should feel free to discuss the treatment options and always check whether any natural remedies you may take will interfere with prescribed medication.

Coughs and Colds

These days we are encouraged to treat minor ailments ourselves – the average cough, cold or sore throat can certainly be alleviated with natural remedies such as this sage, honey and lemon tea.

SAGE, HONEY AND LEMON TEA

1 tbsp honey

300 ml (½ pint) boiling water

15 g (½ oz) red sage leaves

juice of one lemon

Dissolve the honey in the boiling water, then add the red sage leaves and lemon juice. Leave to infuse for 20 minutes. Strain, reheat gently and serve the tea.

A traditional Russian remedy for coughs is to slice three or four large, peeled garlic cloves, place in a bowl and cover with runny honey. Cover the bowl with plastic wrap and leave to infuse for several hours. Take a teaspoon of this surprisingly delicious syrup every couple of hours.

LEFT: HONEY AND LEMON TEA IS A TRADITIONAL REMEDY USED TO TREAT SORE THROATS. SERVE IT IN A PRETTY CHINA CUP WITH A DECORATIVE TWIST OF PEEL TO CHEER AND SOOTHE THE PATIENT.

RIGHT: HONEY HAS LONG BEEN VALUED FOR ITS HEALING AND SOOTHING PROPERTIES. IT IS EASILY DIGESTED AND WILL GIVE A RAPID ENERGY BOOST WHEN NEEDED.

CHEST RUB

Rubbed on to the chest at bedtime, this lotion enriched with soothing
essential oils is both relaxing and acts as a decongestant.

50 ml (2 fl oz) unperfumed body lotion
5 drops frankincense essential oil
5 drops sweet marjoram essential oil
10 drops lavender essential oil

Decant the body lotion into a small bowl and stir in the three essential
oils. As this mixture is stable you can make up a larger quantity for use
as required. Store in an airtight container.

LEFT: CINNAMON BRANDY WAS A POPULAR REMEDY FOR FLU A CENTURY AGO. PLACE HALF A DOZEN CINNAMON STICKS IN A QUARTER BOTTLE OF CHEAP BRANDY AND LEAVE TO INFUSE FOR AT LEAST A WEEK. TAKE ONE OR TWO TEASPOONS IN A LITTLE HOT WATER EVERY HALF HOUR FOR A COUPLE OF HOURS, THEN HOURLY UNTIL YOU FEEL BETTER. A FINAL DOSE AT BEDTIME WILL ALSO HELP YOU TO SLEEP.

Sore Throats

Blackcurrants are very rich in vitamin C and provide an effective remedy for sore throats. For a soothing drink, dissolve a spoonful of blackcurrant jam in a cupful of hot water (pictured left).

Digestive Problems

Herbal teas are among the most effective treatments for indigestion and over-indulgence. Peppermint, thyme, camomile, lemon verbena and fennel are all herbs that soothe. Make the tea by pouring almost boiling water over the fresh herb or tea bag, cover and leave to infuse for at least 5 minutes.

Sore Eyes

Tea bags are convenient and effective treatments for tired or sore eyes. Ordinary tea bags, with their high tannin content, will tighten the skin around the eyes, while camomile is more soothing. Place the tea bags in a saucer or bowl, pour a small amount of almost boiling water over them, cover and leave to infuse and cool. Lie down with the gently squeezed tea bags on your eyes for at least 10 minutes.

To Remove a Splinter from a Finger

Make a strong solution of Epsom salts and water. Soak the finger for as long as possible in the solution – it draws out the splinter and makes it easy to remove.

WINTER WARMER

For a reviving winter pick-me-up, peel and grate
an inch or so of fresh ginger root (shown on the left) into a mug of boiling
water and sweeten with a dash of honey – this make a great
first-thing-in-the-morning drink.

THE
KITCHEN
AND PANTRY

Pots and Pans

In the kitchens of the past, the care of pots and pans was a major chore. These days, non-stick, vitreous enamel and stainless steel finishes have considerably lightened the load, but it is important to choose the correct type of pan for your cooker, and care is still necessary to preserve the surfaces and extend the life of these items. With pots and pans it is well worth buying the best you can afford – good quality cookware can last a lifetime.

Professional cooks always recommend pans with heavy, ground bases as they diffuse the heat evenly and help prevent food sticking and burning. This type of pan is ideal for most types of cookers, the exceptions being halogen hobs, where stainless steel or ceramic pans are recommended, and, of course, microwave ovens, where metal cookware must never be used.

Non-stick Pans

Most of us are familiar with the fact that the technology that brought us the non-stick surface originated from the American space programme, and whatever we may feel about the usefulness of space travel, few would quibble with this particular advance. There is something almost miraculous in the way that a non-stick surface shrugs off anything that comes into contact with it. To ensure that it stays that way it is essential not to use metal implements, which scratch and damage the finish. Instead, use wood, plastic or carbon fibre utensils. Do not use abrasive cleaners on non-stick surfaces.

Which Material?

Cast-iron pans with a vitreous enamel coating are long-lasting and particularly good for Agas and similar cooking ranges. Ideal for casseroles and stews, or any other slow cooking, their major disadvantage is their weight, which can prove unwieldy. In time, the finish inside the pans tends to discolour – this is not a problem

MAKING THE MOST OF CAST-IRON

Provided that cast-iron frying pans, griddles and pancake pans are properly looked after they can be very useful to the serious cook.

When new, cast-iron should be 'seasoned' before use. To do this, paint the surface with vegetable oil and place the pan in a moderate oven for half an hour. Remove from the oven; leave to cool and then repeat the process twice more. To clean the pan, wipe clean with paper towel or wash under hot water, but do not use detergent, which will break down the protective coating.

REMOVING BURNT-ON FOOD

To remove food that has stuck to the bottom of a pan, first fill the pan with a solution of water and biological detergent and leave to stand for a couple of hours. Then bring to the boil. In severe cases it may be necessary to repeat the treatment.

providing the enamel isn't chipped. It can be remedied by filling the pan with a dilute bleach solution, or by rubbing over the surface with a cleaner suitable for enamel baths, but the discoloration will eventually return.

It is hard to better good quality stainless steel pots and pans. The best will have ground bases for efficient heat diffusion and handles which do not conduct the heat. Stainless steel is easy to clean, and can be given an added sparkle occasionally by using a proprietary stainless steel cleaner to remove any dullness.

Few of us use copper in the kitchen these days, and even fewer of us keep it gleaming the way they did in the past, but you may still have a copper whisking bowl or a favourite small pan that you want to keep in good condition. Using a proprietary copper cleaner on something that is used in food preparation can result in tainting. It is far better to use half a lemon, dipped in salt – the effect on tarnishing is quite amazing.

ABOVE: A PLATE RACK PROVIDES USEFUL AND ACCESSIBLE STORAGE FOR YOUR MOST FREQUENTLY USED POTS, PANS AND BAKING TRAYS AS WELL AS PLATES.

RIGHT: IT IS ESSENTIAL THAT ALL PANS USED ON AGAS AND SIMILAR COOKING RANGES HAVE A HEAVY GROUND BASE WHICH SITS FLAT ON THE COOKING PLATES.

China

The word china can mean anything from the finest antique hand-painted porcelain to cheap-and-cheerful crockery bought at a discount store. All china, whether priceless or not, is breakable and needs proper handling if it is to remain in good condition.

China in the Dishwasher

Hand-painted, gilded or silvered china should never be washed in the dishwasher as the heat and the strength of the detergents will quickly damage the patterns. This type of china should always be hand washed. If you are investing in new china, this is something worth bearing in mind. Before you fall madly in love with a particular design, check if it is dishwasher-proof – you may be sentencing yourself (or your nearest and dearest) to many years of servitude in front of the sink. Fortunately, these days, the vast majority of commercially produced china is dishwasher proof, and some has the additional benefit of being ovenproof as well.

Before loading it into a dishwasher, dirty china should be scraped clean and ideally rinsed as well. Load the dishwasher from the back forwards. This ensures that you make good use of all the space available and also cuts down on accidentally chipping the china by knocking one piece against the other as you reach over the plates in the front to try and reach the last remaining space at the back.

Storing China

Storing china on open shelves, dressers or plate racks only really works if the china is used regularly, otherwise there is an inevitable build-up of dust and dirt. This is especially true in the kitchen where fats and oils are convected into the air and mix with

the dust before settling on surfaces and objects. Generally, it is better to store your china in closed cupboards – it needn't be concealed if the cupboards have glass doors, or alternatively, if you have a large kitchen, you can position a dresser or shelves well away from the cooking area where convection is less of a problem.

WHAT TO DO WITH DAMAGED CHINA

Chipped or cracked china should not be used for food as it can harbour germs. Throw it away, use it for mosaics or stand a pot plant on it. Precious china that has suffered damage should be professionally restored, but it will never have the strength of the unbroken item so keep it for display rather than use.

CHINA REGISTRY SERVICES

All too often manufacturers stop making those plates and bowls that you have been using for years but there are china matching services that will track down ends of lines for you (see suppliers' list).

Glass

Some people are habitual glass breakers, while others can own the same set of glasses for years with never a breakage. If you belong to the former category you will probably be well advised to choose robust glasses – like the French style café glasses which, nine times out of ten, will bounce on the floor instead of shattering. Broken glass splinters have the ability to travel vast distances and remain hidden until an unsuspecting person walks barefoot across the floor.

What to put in the Dishwasher

Like china, glass can be divided into two categories – that which can safely be washed in the dishwasher, and that which cannot. Old glass, lead crystal, painted and

LEFT: A COLLECTION OF SMALL VASES AND DRINKING GLASSES PICKED UP FROM JUNK SHOPS AND CAR BOOT SALES CAN BE USED TO DISPLAY SEASONAL FLOWERS PICKED FROM THE GARDEN.

OPPOSITE PAGE: DECORATIVE GLASS IS SEEN TO BEST EFFECT WHEN SPARKLINGLY CLEAN AND DISPLAYED WHERE NATURAL LIGHT CAN SHINE THROUGH IT.

very fragile glass should always be hand-washed. The lead content in old glass and crystal is affected by the heat of the dishwasher, causing the glass to darken and lose its shine. Once washed and rinsed clean, stand it to drain, rim downwards, on a clean cloth before carefully hand drying. Linen glass cloths are preferable for drying glass as they do not leave behind a residue of fluff on the surface.

Some wine connoisseurs advise that detergent should be avoided altogether when washing wine glasses as they believe it may taint the wine, although this does seem to be rather an extreme measure unless you regularly drink the finest vintage wines.

More everyday glassware can safely be washed in the dishwasher. Once again it is best loaded from the back forwards to avoid breakages.

Over time an unattractive 'bloom' may develop on glass that is regularly washed in the dishwasher. Once established this is hard to remove, although you may have some success with limescale remover or an ammonia solution, both of which should be used with great caution. Alternatively, you can delay the build-up by regularly running the dishwasher without detergent when you are washing only glassware.

Storing Glass

Like china, glass is best stored in cupboards rather than on open shelves where dust and dirt are likely to accumulate, and where it is more vulnerable to being knocked over and broken. Good quality glass is worth displaying in a glazed cupboard and the addition of glass shelves and indirect lighting can make an attractive display feature of the glassware.

Cutlery

Few of us have solid silver cutlery these days; even silver-plate is not as popular as it was now that we have neither the time nor the inclination to set aside an hour or so to clean the silver. Most of us want stylish but robust cutlery which can be used every day, but still look good when we are entertaining, and most important of all, emerges from the dishwasher spotlessly clean and in need of no further attention. Alternatively, you could consider owning two sets of cutlery – one for everyday and one for entertaining. Silver or silver-plate that is only used occasionally can be stored in tarnish-proof bags between uses, and if washed and dried carefully (the drying is particularly important), it should only need cleaning twice a year with a long-term silver polish (for full instructions on cleaning silver see page 24).

Storing Cutlery

Everyday cutlery is best stored in an easily accessible cutlery drawer, preferably one that is divided into several compartments. Plastic liners are available for the purpose, but frequently they do not have sufficient compartments, or they aren't long enough, in which case it is worth installing your own drawer dividers. Traditionally these are lined with felt or baize, although silver cutlery should not be stored in felt or baize-lined drawers or boxes as these fabrics give off a tarnishing agent.

Never store kitchen knives among the other cutlery, primarily to avoid injury but also to avoid blunting the blades. A blunt kitchen knife is far more dangerous to use than a sharp one as it is more likely to slip when being used. Store sharp knives in a wooden knife block a rack or on a magnetic strip fixed to the wall, well away from children or where the knives could be accidentally dislodged. Ideally, kitchen knives should be sharpened once a week using a stone, a steel, or a knife sharpener, although this will not work for serrated

knives, which must be professionally sharpened. Where a knife has lost its edge, professional sharpening can restore it, but sharpen it regularly from then on.

CUTLERY IN THE DISHWASHER

Most kitchen knives are best washed by hand, especially those with handles that will be damaged by the dishwasher. However, if you do put sharp knives in the dishwasher be careful to put them in the cutlery holder blade downwards to avoid the possibility of accidents.

Bone-handled and wooden cutlery should not be put in the dishwasher because the heat and detergent will discolour the handles and with old cutlery can loosen the glue that fixes the blade and handle together. Both types of cutlery should be hand-washed in warm water and dried immediately. Wipe over wood or bone with vegetable oil to prevent drying and cracking.

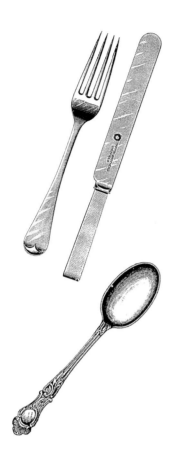

LEFT: SHARP KNIVES SHOULD ALWAYS BE STORED SEPARATELY FROM THE REST OF YOUR CUTLERY, IDEALLY IN A RACK OR BLOCK WELL OUT OF THE REACH OF CHILDREN.

RIGHT: BAMBOO AND OTHER WOODEN-HANDLED CUTLERY SHOULD BE HAND-WASHED IN HOT WATER WITHOUT DETERGENT. OIL THE HANDLES OCCASIONALLY WITH VEGETABLE OIL.

Kitchen Floors

When choosing a kitchen floor, alongside considerations of cost, it is advisable to give some thought to the durability and comfort of your chosen surface. For example, a York stone floor looks wonderful and will last forever, but it is cold to stand on and can be quite tiring on the feet whereas a wood-veneer floor looks good and is warm and comfortable underfoot, but can be damaged by objects dropped on it. If you are the type of person who spends hours in the kitchen you should resist the hard surfaces and choose a type of flooring that is warm as well as easy on the feet. Additionally, you should bear in mind that a stone or tiled floor is very unforgiving of anything that is dropped on it and breakages are much more frequent. Avoid polishing kitchen floors – it makes them slippery, which is particularly dangerous in a kitchen.

Stone Floors

Stone floors are very hard wearing and easy to care for. Dust is removed by sweeping or running the vacuum cleaner over the floor and a weekly wash using a mop and soapy water will remove any other dirt. After washing, use a floor cloth to remove excess water, which may draw out salts from the stone if left unattended and result in marks. An old stone floor will need its lime mortar repointed from time to time to prevent water seeping between the stones and causing damage from below.

Tiled Floors

Like stone floors, tiled floors are best kept clean with a combination of brushing or vacuuming, and then washing with soapy water or a proprietary floor cleaner. Unglazed tiles need to be oiled and sealed when they are first laid or they will absorb water and also stain very easily. This finish will need renewing annually to keep the floor in good condition.

Solid Wood and Wood Veneer Floors

Wooden floors have recently returned to popularity, especially with the advent of modern manufacturing processes. There are three types of flooring available – laminate, which looks like wood but is in fact MDF with a photograph of wood laminated on to it, hardwood veneer on a softwood backing and solid timber. Solid wood, veneer and laminate floors can be swept clean and then washed over with a specially formulated wood wash that cleans without damaging the surface of the floor.

What Price a Wooden Floor?

The price differential between the different types of wooden flooring is large, with laminated wood being the cheapest and solid wood the most expensive. An additional consideration is that laminate and veneer floors can be laid on a solid base without joists and is more stable than natural wood, which shrinks and expands.

Vinyl, Rubber, Linoleum and Marmoleum Floors

These types of flooring are justifiably popular as they are hard-wearing, comfortable underfoot and easy to maintain. Vinyl flooring is the most commonly used, although industrial-type rubber flooring is favoured for high-tech and minimalist kitchens and Linoleum and Marmoleum have recently become popular once again as new designers have experimented with these naturally-derived materials. All these floorings can be mopped clean; rubber scuff marks can be removed by rubbing the mark with an undiluted mild detergent. In addition, Linoleum and Marmoleum should be wiped over with a cloth dipped in a proprietary floor seal once a month in areas of frequent usage, less often elsewhere.

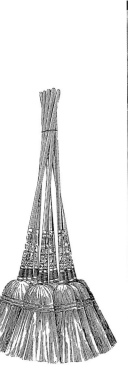

Paintwork

Keeping the kitchen clean is made more difficult by the presence of wet and dry heat, dust, fats and oils, which have a tendency to blend in various combinations and cling to all available surfaces. While other rooms may have one or two of these conditions it is only the kitchen that has the lot. Elsewhere in the home, dusting to keep cobwebs at bay, wiping away fingermarks with a damp cloth and occasionally washing painted woodwork with a diluted detergent will keep paintwork looking fresh, but surfaces in the kitchen generally require more attention.

Surface Protection

Kitchen walls should have a smooth finish, which can be wiped clean. The areas surrounding the cooker, food preparation surfaces and the sink are best tiled or covered with a similar impervious material. Paint the remaining walls with vinyl-silk, eggshell or gloss paint, all of which can be washed down. Similarly, woodwork needs a protective coating of varnish, silk or gloss paint. If the appearance of natural wood appeals to you and you wish to use it in your kitchen, it is advisable either to oil it (use kitchen paper soaked with cooking oil) or to seal it thoroughly with matt-varnish otherwise it will need to be scrubbed to keep it clean.

To keep it looking good between decorating, the paintwork in the kitchen (including the kitchen units), will need washing down from time to time. How often really depends on the size of the kitchen and your style of cooking. If you have a small, poorly-ventilated kitchen and cook a lot of fried food, greasy residue will build up far quicker than in a large kitchen with a powerful extractor fan, or where food is oven-cooked or steamed. These days there is a whole arsenal of suitable kitchen cleaners – cream-based liquids, dirt-dissolving sprays and even anti-bacterial cleaners, all of which will do a good job at routine cleaning. Prior to redecorating the kitchen, or if you inherit a less-than-clean kitchen when you move into a new house, you should wash down all the walls and paintwork with a solution of sugar soap. This will effectively cut through grease and grime and prepare the surface for repainting where applicable.

SUCCESSFUL RE-DECORATING

As tempting as it is to slap on a coat of paint without any preparation of the surface, it will not produce good results, especially in the kitchen, where grease and dust on walls and woodwork will cause poor adhesion. Wash and then rub down woodwork and wash walls before re-painting.

LEFT: KITCHEN WALLS AND WOODWORK
NEED TO BE PAINTED WITH THE CORRECT
TYPE OF PAINT (SEE LEFT) TO ACHIEVE A
DURABLE SURFACE.

RIGHT: HARLEQUIN (UNMATCHED)
KITCHEN CHAIRS LOOK GOOD ALONGSIDE
ONE ANOTHER WHEN PAINTED THE SAME
COLOUR OR TONE.

Windows

Unless your house is located in an exposed area or you experience extreme weather conditions, it is not always obvious when your windows need cleaning. The dirt builds up gradually until a sudden shaft of bright sunlight reveals that your view of the outside world has been fading slowly. Like cleaning a pair of glasses, cleaning windows can bring everything back into sharp focus and brighten colours. In addition, houseplants benefit from the improved daylight, which encourages active growth. For this reason it is important to clean the windows of conservatories and greenhouses regularly.

Cleaning Windows

The easiest way to keep windows clean is simply to employ a window cleaner! A good window cleaner will do the job far quicker and far better than you can. If this option is not available to you, you will have to do them yourself. There are two schools of thought on how to go about this task – there are those who clean one window inside and out every week along with other routine cleaning, and those who do the whole lot once every three months or so. The former method is easier to achieve, while the latter has a more dramatic effect. Which method you choose really depends upon whether you prefer to work methodically through a task or would rather blitz it in one go.

To do a good job you will need a proprietary window cleaning spray and plenty of clean lint-free cloths. You can use old sheeting or T-shirts as cloths or buy window scrim, but whatever you use must be clean or your task will prove more difficult. If the windows are particularly grimy and haven't been cleaned for a while, you can save on cloths by spraying the windows with window cleaner and then using crumpled sheets of newspaper to remove the first layer of dirt. Repeat the process using a clean cloth and your windows will sparkle.

Outside windows that are hard to reach or very large can be cleaned with a telescopic hose attachment available specifically for the purpose. It dispenses a cleaning agent, and cleans quite efficiently, but does tend to leave watermarks as it dries. Once again, employing a window cleaner is the best solution, even if you choose to do the insides yourself.

EFFICIENT CLEANING METHODS

Two tried-and-tested methods for cleaning your windows make use of newspaper and vinegar. Newspaper is a very efficient way of removing the initial grime – the paper absorbs all that water and it is a good way of using up all those piles of paper that tend to lie around the home. Finish the cleaning with a diluted solution of vinegar, which is a most effective way of cutting through any grease that may have accumulated on the window.

To Prevent Windows Steaming-up

*Soak a clean duster in a strong detergent solution and
allow it to dry without rinsing it out. Wipe over clean
windows with the duster and they will remain clear
even in the steamiest of kitchens.*

IF AN OPEN WINDOW REVEALS THAT THE WORLD IS A MUCH
BRIGHTER PLACE THAN IT APPEARS THROUGH THE CLOSED
WINDOW, YOU WILL KNOW FOR SURE THAT IT IS TIME TO
GIVE THE GLASS A THOROUGH CLEAN.

Fruit

Fruit appears to come in two categories – the fruit which is so popular that it disappears within hours of being bought, and the rest that sit in the fruit bowl until they rot, or are rescued at the last moment and made into fruit salad or crumble. Neither of these categories is fixed – the clementines which the children could not get enough of last week suddenly go out of favour just as you buy them in industrial quantities and they will be clamouring instead for something you neglected to purchase.

There is no easy answer to this dilemma, but a certain amount of 'fruit management' will cut down on wastage. A large bowl overflowing with fruit is decorative to look at, but it does invite waste. An alternative is to keep the majority of your fruit (with the exception of bananas – see below) in the fridge and have a small bowl containing a few pieces of fruit on the table. As the fruit is eaten it can be replenished.

Different Ways with Different Fruit

Soft fruit such as strawberries, cherries, raspberries and blackberries should all be stored unwashed in the fridge – once they have been washed they need to be either eaten within a few hours, lightly cooked or sprinkled with sugar, otherwise they will start to deteriorate. Melon, too, benefits from being stored in the fridge once it has been cut although it is best to leave it at room temperature while it is still ripening.

Ripe stone fruit, which includes plums, peaches, apricots and nectarines, and citrus fruit should be stored either in a cool place or in the refrigerator, but fruit that is still hard will need to be kept in a warm place to complete the ripening process. A ripe fruit put in among unripe fruit will speed up this process.

Orchard fruit – apples, pears, quinces – can be stored for some time in a cool larder or store room, provided the fruit is unblemished and the different fruits are kept separately, or they will tend to taint one another. They can be placed on slatted wooden shelves; individually wrapped in newspaper, or packed into plastic bags, which have been pierced to prevent the fruit sweating. Whichever method you use, you should check the fruit regularly and remove any that show signs of deterioration as this will quickly spread to the other fruit.

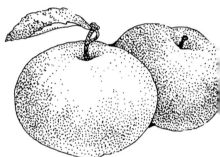

BANANAS

Always store bananas separately from other fruit as the gas they give off as they ripen shortens the life of the other fruit. Of course, if you have fruit that needs to ripen more quickly, popping it in a paper bag with a banana will speed up the process. The skin of bananas blackens if they are stored below 12.5°C and the flesh becomes woody, so don't keep bananas in the fridge.

Vegetables

In the days when nearly everyone grew their own vegetables, the storing of vegetables was a time-consuming process which ensured a continuity of fresh produce throughout the year. Root vegetables were stored outdoors in clamps, or in cellars; the summer harvest was bottled, pickled, salted or dried; and seasonal vegetables were picked fresh from the garden as they were needed.

These days, few of us rely exclusively (or at all) on our gardens for produce; we buy most of our vegetables washed clean of soil, pre-packaged, and even chopped ready for use. Sadly, what is gained in convenience is often sacrificed in flavour and nutrition. The vitamin content of many vegetables does not remain stable after they have been harvested, particularly once they have been washed and prepared. It may surprise you to know that frozen vegetables often have better vitamin levels than their 'fresh' alternatives. Green vegetables, such as peas, beans, brassicas and leaf vegetables, should all be stored in the fridge, preferably unwashed.

Salads

Nutritionally, the best salads are those that have just been picked from the garden. Failing that, try to buy them in a condition as close to their natural state as possible, i.e. whole, unwashed lettuces, untrimmed celery, bunched watercress. Pre-washed, pre-packaged salads are convenient, time-saving and often contain a variety of ingredients which it would not be economical to buy separately, but they should be eaten on the day of purchase or they will contribute little to your diet. All green salad vegetables are best stored in a cool place, ideally the crisper drawer of your fridge. Mushrooms are the other vegetable to keep in this drawer, but don't wash them until you are going to use them and also store the mushrooms in a paper bag to keep them dry.

Tomatoes

The smell and taste of a freshly-picked ripe tomato is one of life's delights. Follow the example of the best chefs and keep your tomatoes in a bowl on the kitchen counter rather than in the fridge – this retains and even improves the flavour.

Root Vegetables

Root vegetables are best stored unwashed in a cool larder, but given that most of us buy them ready-washed from the supermarket, and few of us have larders these days, they should be stored in the vegetable drawer of the fridge.

Potatoes

There was a time when potatoes came in two categories – new and main crop. New potatoes were a delicacy to be savoured for an all too short season, before moving on to the main crop, which would be used the rest of the year. Now a quick look at the supermarket shelves reveals a huge range of choices all year round. Like other root vegetables, the best potatoes nutritionally are those that have not been previously washed, and are cooked with their skins intact, even if they are removed after cooking. Potatoes should always be stored in a cool, dark place with good ventilation.

Onions, Shallots, Garlic

Strings of these vegetables are decorative, but also functional as they need good air circulation to remain in the best condition. Alternatively, they can be stored in wire baskets. They should not be kept in the fridge.

Squashes, Marrows, Pumpkins

All of these vegetables can be eaten young or stored for winter-eating. To store successfully, they should be left to mature on the plant and then ripen in a well-ventilated place. As they mature, the skin will harden and the flesh deepen in colour, taking on a nutty flavour.

Jams

People who have never made jam tend to think that it is a difficult, complicated process requiring specialist knowledge and equipment. It isn't. It is true that making marmalade, for instance, can be time-consuming and requires a number of different steps – boiling the fruit, removing the pith, chopping the skins. But it is also true that with 500 g (1 lb) of strawberries and 500 g (1 lb) of jam sugar you can make 1 kg (2 lb) of jam in under half an hour.

You can make jam with any kind of sugar, but the novice (and those with busy lives) will appreciate the reliability and speed offered by jam sugar. Jam sugar has added apple pectin (the setting agent) and tartaric acid. This means that jam will reach setting point after 4 minutes of a rolling boil, which is when the jam continues boiling when you stir it, rather than subsiding. Although this type of sugar is more expensive than ordinary preserving sugar, the speedy results and the freshness of the jam's flavour justifies the expense. Jam made this way does not last as long as ordinary jams and should be refrigerated after the jar is opened, but shelf life is not really a problem when the jam is so easy to make. Fruit can be picked or bought when it is at its best, some can be made into jam immediately and the rest can be frozen for later jam-making.

Fruits contain differing levels of natural pectins – a naturally occurring setting agent. Those high in pectin include gooseberries, apples, damsons, blackcurrants and redcurrants, while strawberries, cherries, blackberries and rhubarb are all low in pectin. The pectin level in any fruit will drop as it ripens, so jam is best made with slightly under-ripe fruit. When using preserving sugar or other types of sugar, you can raise the pectin levels by adding lemon juice or fruit naturally high in pectin.

Jam Jars

It is essential that the jars used for jam-making are clean and dry before they are used, and that they are warm when they are filled or they may crack. If you have a dishwasher you can do this by putting the jars and their lids through a hot cycle (they must be completely dry as well). Alternatively, wash the jars in hot, soapy water, rinse them and then place them upside down on a rack in a moderately warm oven for 30 minutes to dry and heat through while you are making the jam. If the jam is not going to be eaten immediately, put lids on top of the jars to keep the interior sterile.

QUICK JAM

500 g (1 lb) prepared soft fruit

500 g (1 lb) jam sugar

Clean, dry, warmed jam jars

Waxed paper discs

A small plate or saucer, chilled in the freezer (to test for setting point)

Place the sugar in a bowl and put in the oven to warm through (with the jars). Put the fruit in a large, heavy-based saucepan over a very low heat, stirring gently until the juice starts to run. Stir in the warmed sugar and keep stirring until the sugar and fruit mixture liquifies. Increase the heat and bring to a rolling boil for 4 minutes. Remove from heat.

Pour a teaspoon of the jam on to the chilled plate – wait a minute and then gently push it with your finger. If a wrinkled skin forms it is ready; if not, boil for another minute or two and re-test. Leave the jam to stand for 15 minutes and then stir to disperse the fruit evenly through the jam. Pour the jam into the warmed jars, cover the surface with waxed discs and replace the lids once the jam has cooled.

Jellies

The main difference between jams and jellies is that jams generally contain the entire fruit, while jellies are made from the juice that has been strained off the cooked fruit before sugar is added. The resulting syrup is then heated to setting point. Jam is dense and opaque, while well-made jelly should be translucent and crystal clear. Another difference is that unlike jams, jellies are not solely used at breakfast and tea time; they are also a traditional accompaniment to roast meat. Use mint or redcurrant jelly with lamb; cranberry jelly with turkey; thyme or tarragon-flavoured apple jelly with chicken; crab apple jelly with pork; blackcurrant jelly with duck, and rowan jelly is delicious with most roast meats, including game. A spoonful of the appropriate jelly added to the gravy will further enhance the flavour.

Making Jelly

Making jelly is not as quick as jam making, because of the necessary interruption while you wait for the juice to strain from the fruit, which is best done overnight, but the results are definitely worth the effort. Although you can strain the fruit through an old (but clean) pillowcase, a piece of muslin or a tea towel, you would be well-advised to invest in an inexpensive jelly bag and stand. These will make your life much easier as they eliminate the frequently messy business of searching around for a suitable hook to suspend the pulp from, and the lengthy adjustments that ensue as you position the bowl underneath.

Apple jelly is one of the easiest to make, sets reliably and is the basis for a number of herb-flavoured jellies including mint jelly, which is made by adding finely chopped mint to the jelly once setting point has been reached.

APPLE JELLY

1 kg (2¼ lb) apples

Water

Jelly bag and stand

Warmed jam sugar

Clean, dry, warmed jam jars

Waxed paper discs

A small plate or saucer, chilled in the freezer (to test for setting point)

Wash the apples and chop roughly, removing any bruised or blemished areas, but do not peel or core. Place in a large pan and just cover with cold water. Bring to the boil then lower the heat and simmer until soft. Strain the pulp through a jelly bag – this is best done overnight. Resist the temptation to try and squeeze more juice from the pulp as this will cloud the jelly. Measure the juice into a heavy-based saucepan and for every 600 ml (1 pint) add 450 g (1 lb) of warmed jam sugar. Heat gently until the sugar has dissolved, raise the heat until a rolling boil is achieved and then boil for 4 minutes. Test for setting (see page 86). Pour into warmed, clean, dry jam jars. Cover the jelly with waxed paper discs and replace the lids.

Pickles

In the past, when Monday was the day that most households ate the leftovers from Sunday lunch, home-made pickles were an essential accompaniment to cold meat. Nowadays, few of us eat Sunday's leftovers on Monday, and even fewer of us make our own pickles. This is a pity because they are easy to make and taste far better than most commercially produced pickles.

A pickle is usually made from vegetables or fruit, which are preserved in spiced vinegar or brine. There are two types of pickle. First, there those that involve cooking the fruit or vegetables in the pickling mix. And, second, there are those, like pickled onions, where the hot pickling mix is poured on to the uncooked onions, which have been packed into a sterilized jar – this results in the characteristic crunch of the pickled onion, which would not be there had it been cooked.

Crunchy Pickled Onions

675 g (1½ lb) pickling onions or shallots

3 x 500 g (1 lb) jars

Bay leaves

600 ml (1 pint) malt vinegar

175 g (6 oz) brown sugar

50 g (2 oz) sea salt

2 tsp pickling spice

Put the onions or shallots in a large bowl and pour boiling water over them to loosen the skins. Peel the onions and pack into warmed, sterilized jars (see page 93). Add a bay leaf to each jar. Bring the vinegar, sugar, salt and pickling spice to the boil, stirring until the sugar has dissolved, and then pour the mixture over the onions and seal immediately. The onions will be ready to eat in two weeks.

Pickle Precautions

Pickling mixes must not be boiled up in aluminium saucepans, which can react with the vinegars, and the pickles should be stored in wide-mouthed, glass-lidded preserving jars to ensure that the pickling mix does not come into contact with any metal, as harmful corrosion could take place.

Pear Pickle

If you have ever wondered what to do with bullet-hard pears, this pear pickle will solve your problem. With their sweet-sour flavour they make the perfect accompaniment to thick slices of country ham served with buttery mashed potatoes.

1 kg (2¼ lb) hard pears

Juice of 2 lemons

675 g (1½ lb) demerara sugar

1 litre (1¾ pints) cider vinegar

250 ml (8 fl oz) water

3 cinnamon sticks

3 whole star anise

1 tsp whole black peppercorns

1 tsp whole allspice

Clean, dry, warmed pickling jars

Peel the pears and toss them in lemon juice. Measure the rest of the ingredients into a large saucepan, add the pears and bring to the boil. Reduce the heat and simmer until the pears are cooked through but not soft (30-45 minutes). Spoon the pickled pears into warmed sterilized jars (see page 93) and seal immediately.

Bottling

Before the advent of freezers, bottling was the most common method of preserving food for winter use. Long, hot, summer and autumn days were spent transforming the abundant harvest of the garden into rows of bottled fruit and vegetables; the opportunity could not be missed or the family would go hungry later on. Fortunately, our family's health and well-being no longer depend on our skills at bottling but by using these techniques, a glut of fruit or tomatoes can be transformed into something far superior to anything we can buy.

Various types of bottling jars are available, all made from robust, heat-proof glass with a wide neck. Some have a glass lid, a rubber ring and metal clamps, which hold the lid in place, while others have a lid in two parts, a flat metal disc and a screw lid. Depending on the type of jar, the rubber ring or the metal disc must be replaced each time the jars are used for bottling to ensure a safe and secure seal. The bottling process involves packing fruit or vegetables into jars in syrup, brine or their own juices. The jars and their contents are then sterilized by one of two methods: a water-bath or in the oven.

Water-bath Sterilizing

First place a wooden trivet or a folded cloth at the bottom of a large lidded saucepan. Stand the sealed jars in the pan and fold cloths around them to prevent them touching. Fill the pan with cold water until the bottles are covered by at least 2.5 cm (1 in) of water and bring the water to the boil and then simmer for 40 minutes. Allow the water to cool until you can safely remove the jars to a dry surface (this prevents the jars cracking). Then leave them overnight – as the jars cool, a vacuum forms. The next day, test the seals by removing the clamps and gently lifting each jar by its lid. If the seal does not hold, the food should be eaten within a few days.

Oven Sterilizing

First line a baking tray with a thick layer of newspaper. Then stand the jars on the tray with the lids resting on the jars, but not sealed, and place them in a low oven (120°C/250°F/Gas ½). After 45 minutes, check if the liquid in the jars can be seen to be simmering. If so, remove the jars from the oven and seal immediately. If not, wait a further 5 minutes and check once again. The following day, when the jars have fully cooled, test the seals (see above).

OVEN-BOTTLED TOMATOES

Ripe tomatoes

Clean, dry, warmed bottling jars

Garlic

Fresh basil leaves

Whole black peppercorns

Sea salt

Peel the tomatoes and tightly pack them into clean, dry bottling jars adding peeled cloves of garlic and bay leaves and a sprinkling of peppercorns and sea salt as you fill the jar. Leave the neck of the jar clear to allow space for the vacuum to form. Carefully wipe the rim of the jar and replace the lid, but do not fasten. Follow the instructions above for oven sterilizing.

YOU DON'T NEED A GLUT OF PRODUCE, OR EVEN A GARDEN, TO BOTTLE FOOD. GIVE BOUGHT OLIVES EXTRA ZIP BY REPLACING THE ORIGINAL BRINE WITH YOUR OWN, WHICH YOU HAVE FLAVOURED WITH CHILLIES AND OTHER SPICES. QUARTERED LEMONS PACKED TIGHTLY INTO A PRESERVING JAR WITH LAYERS OF SEA SALT, BAY LEAVES AND CINNAMON STICKS WILL TRANSFORM INTO THE SALTED LEMONS USED IN MOROCCAN COOKERY. OVER A PERIOD OF 3-4 WEEKS THE JUICES WILL SOFTEN AND PRESERVE THE PEEL. ALWAYS REMEMBER TO USE SPOTLESSLY CLEAN JARS.

Oils and Vinegars

Over the last 25 years our use and understanding of oils and vinegars has undergone a revolution. Prior to that, olive oil was a pale yellow liquid bought from chemists for the treatment of earache, and malt vinegar was sprinkled on bags of chips. With the advent of supermarkets and the globalization of food, we now seek out estate-bottled, cold-pressed extra virgin olive oils as eagerly as fine wines, and the once rare balsamic vinegar is used on everything from rocket salad to strawberries.

Oils

Having sought out fine oils, don't be tempted to squirrel them away in the back of a cupboard to be brought out on rare occasions. Unprocessed oils (which these are) have a limited shelf life and they are considered to be at their best six weeks to two months after pressing, when the acidity which is present at first has mellowed, but the full flavour is still there to be appreciated. Over the following months the oil will mellow further and it should be used by the next harvest. Use your best olive oil cold on salads, drizzled over roasted

vegetables or on freshly cooked spaghetti and cook instead with a good quality, medium-priced supermarket oil. Store good olive oil in a cool, dark place – not on the worktop next to the stove. The same is true of all cold-pressed oils – the nut oils in particular tend to go rancid after six months or so. Sesame oil also deteriorates quite rapidly so keep a careful eye on the use-by date. Ordinary cooking oils are less fussy.

Around Christmas time the shelves of shops are crowded with decorative bottles of oil flavoured with herbs, garlic and spices. These may look good, but they sometimes contain poor oils and inferior flavourings. They are easy to make at home, but because of recent concerns about the potential for food poisoning, it is recommended that the flavourings should be removed from the oil after they have macerated for 1-2 weeks.

Spicy Pizza Oil

This is the oil for those who like their pizza with a bit of a kick. Drizzle it over the hot pizza just before you eat it.

500 ml (17 fl oz) virgin olive oil
2 small fresh green chillies
4 small fresh red chillies
3 cloves of garlic
Small bunch of thyme
1 tbsp black peppercorns
Clean, dry, warmed bottle

Slice the green chillies into thin rings and peel the garlic and cut into slivers. Put the sliced chillies, garlic and all other ingredients in a previously sterilized bottle (see page 87). Seal the bottle with a clean, dry cork and leave to stand for 10-14 days. Shake the bottle occasionally to blend the flavours. Strain off the flavourings and store the oil in a cool place in a clean, dry bottle.

Vinegars

Vinegar has enjoyed a similar renaissance to that of oil; wine vinegar is now more used than malt vinegar, and cider vinegar is appreciated as being more robust than wine vinegar but less harsh than malt. As a natural preservative, vinegar needs less delicate handling than oil and certainly does not need to be kept under special conditions. Balsamic vinegar and sherry vinegar can be used to add a sweet-sour flavour to dressings and sauces, but should be used with a light hand or they can overwhelm. Flavoured vinegars are easily made at home, but like the oils, the flavourings should be removed once they have infused.

Tarragon Vinegar

600 ml (1 pint) white wine vinegar
6 tbsp chopped fresh tarragon
1 tsp black peppercorns

Heat the vinegar to boiling point and pour over the tarragon. Cover and leave to macerate for three days. Strain the vinegar into a clean, dry bottle and seal with a cork.

Herbs and Spices

Throughout history, herbs and spices have been used to flavour foods. In the past, when food was often less-than-fresh, herbs and spices were essential both to disguise unpleasant flavours and to

offer some protection via their medicinal qualities. Most herbs were introduced to Britain through the monasteries where the medicinal herb gardens were initially used solely for treating illness. But gradually the food enhancing qualities of the herbs came to be appreciated and the local populace started to grow them in their own kitchen gardens. Spices were traded with the East and were considered so valuable that the mistress of the household would keep them under lock and key to be handed out in strictly controlled amounts.

Handling Herbs

Today, fresh herbs are readily available all the year round, cut and ready-for-use or growing in pots, which can be kept on the kitchen windowsill, but many of us still enjoy growing our own herbs for drying and preserving. Harvest herbs early on a sunny day, after the dew has evaporated, but before midday. This may sound rather mystical, but there is a scientific reason for this. Mid-morning is the time when the herbs are dry, and the volatile oils are at their most concentrated. Any earlier, and the herbs will still be damp, and later on in the day the oils start to evaporate into the surrounding air. After picking, wrap the herbs in cones of newspaper and hang them upside down in an airy place until they are fully dry. Once the herbs are dry, remove them from their paper cones and store them in glass jars in a cool, dark place.

Herbs at their Best

Dried herbs will remain in good condition for a year, but it is advisable to throw away the remnants of last year's herbs annually and replace them with newly dried herbs if you are going to enjoy them at their best.

Spices

Spices are best stored whole – once a spice has been ground it will slowly lose both its aroma and its flavour. Like herbs, they should be kept in a cool place away from direct light. To enjoy the full flavour of spices, use them freshly ground – an electric coffee grinder is ideal for this purpose. Clean it between using it for different spices by grinding a couple of teaspoons of rock salt. The salt will pick up any spice residues and leave the grinder untainted.

LEFT: HARVEST HOME-GROWN HERBS REGULARLY THROUGHOUT THE GROWING SEASON TO PROVIDE A PLENTIFUL SUPPLY AND KEEP THE PLANTS PRODUCING NEW SHOOTS.

RIGHT: WHOLE SPICES SUCH AS CLOVES OR CINNAMON STICKS CAN BE TIED INTO SMALL MUSLIN BUNDLES, WHICH ALLOW THEM TO BE EASILY REMOVED FROM STEWS AND CASSEROLES ONCE THEY HAVE IMPARTED THEIR FLAVOURS.

Wines

Wine has become an everyday drink. Now that most of us choose to drink a glass of wine with our evening meal, it is no longer saved for special occasions, or meals out. Our choice of wine is generally dictated by individual taste preferences and, of course, price. There is a great deal of snobbery and mystique about wine, but as its enjoyment is largely subjective you should trust your own palate and make your choice accordingly. If you lack the confidence to do this, be guided by the experts; read the columnists and make a note of their recommended wines – buy the wine and see if you agree. If you do, it will encourage you to follow future recommendations. Bear in mind that a well-chosen, inexpensive wine often tastes better than a pricey wine from a poor vintage, which may be all style and no substance.

One of the best ways to learn more about wine is to take a course in wine appreciation. Knowledgeable tutors will explain the characteristics of various wines and help you learn to differentiate and discriminate – a process that is both informative and fun!

Storing Wine

Once you have got the wine home it is important that you treat it well if it is going to taste its best. All wine – red,

ANY WINE THAT IS TO BE KEPT FOR MORE THAN A WEEK OR SO SHOULD BE STORED LYING DOWN IN A DARK AND COOL (BUT NOT COLD) PLACE.

white and rose – should be stored lying on its side in a cool dark place unless it is going to be drunk within a week. Kitchen wine racks are usually far too warm to keep the wine in good condition and certainly shouldn't be used for long-term storage.

To allow the full flavour of red wines to develop they should be brought into a warm room and uncorked at least four hours before serving. Rapid warming, e.g. standing wine next to the fire or the cooker, is not recommended.

White wines need to be chilled for an hour before serving, or can be chilled more rapidly using a sleeve, which is kept in the freezer when not in use. The flavour and aroma of white wine is blunted if the wine is too cold and chilling it in the freezer is not recommended. Quality white wines and champagnes should not be kept in the fridge, rather they should be stored alongside other wines and then be chilled as needed.

Stop the Deterioration

Once wine has been opened, the contents can be kept in good condition by using a rubber stopper which is used with a pump to remove the air from the bottle and prevent deterioration. Special champagne stoppers clip around the neck of the bottle and keep the bubbles bubbly. An open bottle of champagne will retain its bubbles overnight in the fridge without a stopper.

Syrups, Cordials and Ratafias

In the days before there were supermarket shelves laden with carbonated drinks, cartons of juice and bottled mineral waters, people relied on home-made syrups and cordials for everyday drinks. Favourite recipes were handed down from one generation to the next and family outings were arranged to gather the fruit or flowers, which were the essential ingredients.

Making Syrups and Cordials

A few households still make fresh lemonade and ginger beer for hot summer days and harvest elderflowers to make a delicious and delicate cordial. The taste of these drinks is a world away from the commercially produced drinks we are used to. The making of ginger beer at home should be approached with some caution, however, as the mixture is very active in the bottles and can explode! The following recipes for lemonade and elderflower cordial are non-explosive and quite delicious.

LEMONADE
....

This is a wonderfully thirst-quenching drink, best made the
evening before it is to be consumed.

4 unwaxed, preferably organic, lemons
50 g (2 oz) sugar
1.5 litres (3 pints) boiling water

Pare the lemons very thinly. Place the lemon rinds and sugar in a large
jug and pour on the boiling water. Leave to cool and then strain.
Squeeze the lemons and add their juice. Serve chilled.

ELDERFLOWER CORDIAL

1.5 litres (2½ pints) boiling water

1.5 kg (3 lb) granulated sugar

50 g (2 oz) citric acid

25 elderflower heads washed and shaken dry

2 unwaxed, preferably organic, sliced lemons

Clean, dry, warmed bottles

Dissolve the sugar in the boiling water and leave to cool. When cool, stir in the citric acid, elderflowers and sliced lemons. Cover and leave to macerate for 3 days, stirring occasionally. Strain and pour into clean, sterilized bottles (see page 87). Seal. Store in a cool place where it will keep indefinitely. Serve diluted to taste with still or sparkling mineral water.

Ratafias

Ratafias are the alcoholic version of syrups and cordials. They are an easy and delicious way of transforming a glut of soft fruit into an after-dinner liqueur to drink at your own table or take along instead of the ubiquitous bunch of flowers when you are invited to friends. Ratafias can be made with any soft fruit such as raspberries, strawberries, tayberries, mulberries and blackberries, but resist mixing them unless you like the idea of summer pudding ratafia!

MAKING A RATAFIA

Ratafias are made by volume rather than weight, and depend on the amount of fruit available.

Fill a previously sterilized wide-mouthed, lidded jar with the fruit (see page 87). Add caster sugar until it reaches one third of the way up the jar. Pour on vodka until the jar is full. Seal and shake to help dissolve the sugar. Store in a cool, dark place for two months, shaking the jar occasionally. Strain off the fruit (delicious but powerful) and bottle the ratafia in clean, dry, sterilized bottles. It will keep indefinitely.

Dealing with Pests

Flies

On the whole, flies may only be a minor irritation rather than a major pest, but nonetheless they are a health hazard and even a single fly can drive you to distraction as it buzzes against a window or persistently lands on you. Flies do not like strongly aromatic herbs, so growing them beneath windows or placing pots of them on windowsills can help to repel flies. There is a traditional belief that flies are averse to the colour blue – in Holland stables are traditionally painted blue inside to keep flies away from the horses – so it may be worth experimenting with this colour if you have a persistent problem. More pragmatically, the old-fashioned sticky fly-papers may not be pretty to look at, but they are very effective without any of the potential problems of chemical fly sprays.

Carpet Beetle

The carpet beetle loves dirt and dark places. The best way to prevent an infestation is to vacuum thoroughly and regularly, using attachments to reach right up to the skirting and under furniture. The early stage of the insect, known as a 'woolly bear', is very active and will leave holes spread over a large area.

Moths

Moths are not just a pest in fabrics, they can also infest dry goods such as breakfast cereals, grains, pulses and pasta. Once established in the kitchen they can be hard to eradicate as they spread quickly through opened packets and will even make their way into jars with

screw-top lids. Really the only solution is a thorough spring clean. Throw away any dried foods, herbs, nuts, flour and dried fruit packs that have been opened or were not adequately sealed in the first place. Wash down the cupboards and in future be sure to store any opened packets in jars or boxes with tightly fitting lids.

Fleas

If you have pets you will be extremely fortunate if you don't have an occasional flea infestation. This is most common in the autumn when the central heating is first switched on after the summer and the fleas take to the carpets and then leap on any passing ankle. This is certainly a case where prevention is much better, and far less time consuming, than the cure. Treat your pets regularly with a flea treatment recommended by your vet and you should not have any problems. Once fleas are established indoors, vacuuming with a powerful vacuum cleaner will control a minor infestation, but if the problem persists you will need to call in a pest control officer.

Wasps

You should not attempt to deal with a wasps' nest yourself. Always call in a pest control officer who will be able to eradicate the problem without endangering your family or himself.

Headlice

Few homes with school-age children are free of this menace. Now that most chemical remedies have been discredited, daily combing of conditioner-drenched hair with a nit comb is recommended. It is essential to removes eggs as well as the nits to banish an infestation.

Pet Care

The theory is that pets teach children responsibility but the reality is that they more often seem to reveal how swiftly children learn to evade responsibility! Bear this in mind when choosing a pet: start small, with a rodent of limited lifespan or a goldfish which can be liberated in a garden pond, and only move on to larger creatures if you are confident that the children are up to it, or if you are happy to undertake all the care required. A pet should be a loved member of the family, not the cause of endless arguments.

Rodents

Rats, hamsters and gerbils all make good first pets for children. None live more than two years and they are generally trouble-free. A reputable pet shop will sell you the correct equipment and advise you on feed when you buy the rodent. Children should be encouraged to handle the pet daily, or it will become less sociable and the children will quickly lose interest. It is essential that children wash their hands thoroughly after handling rodents.

Goldfish

A goldfish bowl should only ever be a temporary home for goldfish – it is too small to be a permanent home. Buy goldfish from a reputable source and ask advice about aquarium size, plants, pump, etc. The shop will be keen to sell you all sorts of accessories, but start with just the essentials or your two tiddlers may turn into a major investment. Overfeeding is the major cause of problems with goldfish, clouding and fouling the water and sometimes causing premature death. Clean out the tank once a month, transferring the fish to a temporary home with some water from the tank. The freshly-filled tank should be left to reach room temperature before replacing the fish and if tap water is used, a chemical must be added to remove the chlorine.

Cats

One of the top two pets, alongside dogs, cats can be kept in situations which would be unsuitable for a dog. However, a cat that never experiences the freedom of outdoors is not living the life it was intended to live. With their independent nature they are ideal pets for working people. A cat flap allows them to go in and out at will and, if you are lucky, they will be pleased to see you when you get home, especially if your arrival signals a mealtime. Although they lack the devotion of a dog, they are affectionate: a purring cat settled on a lap is a pleasure for cat and cat-lover alike.

Rabbits

Parents often choose a rabbit as a compromise when a child really wants a dog or a cat. This is most likely to work if it is a house rabbit, so can live indoors. House rabbits are increasingly popular as they are sociable and entertaining companions, which can be successfully house-trained. Regular grooming and plenty of handling will stop them developing anti-social habits such as biting and scratching. Unfortunately, they do have a tendency to chew on wires, so they should be restricted to areas where wiring is out of their reach. Never pick up a rabbit by its ears.

Dogs

As the adverts remind us, a dog is not just for Christmas. They can be loving and devoted companions, but they can also be dirty, noisy, and smelly and require exercising daily for an average of ten years. This is quite a commitment and should not be lightly undertaken. However, as long as you are aware of the pitfalls in advance, the rewards will far outweigh the responsibilities. Good training and regular exercise will help keep your dog healthy, happy and socialized, ensuring that it mixes well with people and other dogs. A dog should always have its own bed, a resting place and refuge that is respected as such by the rest of the household. Traditional wicker baskets remain popular, but Labradors and other 'chewy' dogs can quickly destroy them. The modern bean-bag dog bed is a comfortable, durable and hygienic alternative. Whatever type of bed you choose, it and any bedding should be washed regularly to keep it and your dog smelling sweet.

DOG AND CAT CARE

Grooming keeps a dog's coat in good condition, with occasional baths when the dog smells too antisocial. Long-haired cats should be groomed frequently, too, as severe skin infections can result if this is neglected. To keep a cat or dog healthy it is also essential that they are vaccinated annually, given flea-treatment regularly and any illness is treated without delay.

THE
LAUNDRY

Stain Removal

Every laundry should have a stain removal kit, ready for immediate action when the need arises. The quicker a stain is treated, the more likely it is that it will be successfully removed, so having the necessary ingredients to hand makes good sense. When removing a stain, always work from the outside of the stain to the centre to prevent it spreading.

A Basic Stain Removal Kit

a roll of white absorbent paper towels

clean, soft white cloths

nail brush

spatula

bleach

ammonia

colour-run remover

pre-soaker

biological detergent

a proprietary grease solvent

salt

glycerine solution (equal parts glycerine and water)

non-oily nail varnish remover

methylated spirits

specialist stain removers (e.g. ballpoint or felt-tip pen)

white spirit

white vinegar

Treating a Stain

How you treat a stain depends on what has caused it. Food and drink stains can often be soaked away, while inks and cosmetics need suitable solvents to shift them. Always check the care labels on a garment before using bleaches or specialist stain removers, and if in doubt, test the stain remover on a concealed part of the garment. Wool and silk must not be soaked. Instead, where soaking is recommended to remove a stain, replace this treatment with sponging the garment using a solution made up of equal parts of water and glycerine. Precious garments and fine fabrics are best treated by a specialist cleaner – attempts to remove stains at home can often inflict more damage than the original stain.

Ballpoint pen: Remove using a proprietary product or a cotton bud dipped in methylated spirits. Launder as usual.

Blood: Initially soak in salted cold water, then in a biological detergent solution before laundering.

Chewing gum: Fold small garments in a plastic bag and place in the freezer until the gum has hardened and can be chipped off. Treat larger garments by placing a bag of ice cubes on to the gum until it has hardened. Remove any residue by sponging with warm water.

Chocolate: Carefully scrape off any residue and then launder in a biological detergent.

Coffee: Rinse in warm water and then soak in biological detergent before washing as usual.

Cosmetics: Oil-based cosmetics such as foundation, lipstick and mascara should be removed with cottonwool soaked with some white spirit before laundering. Nail polish should be removed using a non-oily nail varnish remover before washing the garment.

THERE IS NO STANDARD
WAY TO TREAT A STAIN — IT
DEPENDS ON WHAT HAS
CAUSED THE STAIN AND
THE TYPE OF FABRIC.
WRONG TREATMENT CAN
SET A STAIN SO THAT IT
BECOMES PERMANENT, BUT
CORRECT TREATMENT WILL
LEAVE THE FABRIC LOOKING
AS GOOD AS NEW.

Curry: This is one of the more stubborn stains and professional cleaning will be necessary for non-washable fabrics. Washable fabrics should be soaked in warm water, changing the water when necessary. Drain and squeeze out excess water. Apply a mixture of equal parts glycerine and water to the stain and leave for an hour. Rinse, repeat if needed and then launder in a biological detergent.

Dye-runs: We have all experienced that sinking feeling when opening the washing machine door to find that a load of white laundry has turned a dirty grey colour thanks to a fugitive non-colourfast item which had concealed itself in the drum from a previous load. Prevention is always better than cure. Check the drum before loading a white wash, sort the laundry carefully to ensure that no coloured items are included and use a proprietary colour catcher (see suppliers' list). Included in a white wash, this cloth will efficiently mop up any dye and prevent it discolouring your white laundry. For laundry that has already been discoloured, immediately put it through another cycle, including a proprietary colour run remover for coloured items or a laundry whitener for a white load. If this fails to work, soaking in a biological detergent can sometimes help, while a bleach solution can brighten whites.

Egg: Remove raw egg by soaking in biological detergent; cooked egg stains should be soaked in salted water, rinsed, soaked in plain water and then laundered.

Felt-tip pen: Dab up any excess using a paper towel then treat with a proprietary stain remover or cotton buds dipped in methylated spirits. Launder.

Fruit juices: Rinse in cold running water before laundering using biological detergent.

Grass: Launder using a biological detergent. For stubborn stains, dab with methylated spirits before washing again.

Grease and oil: Treat delicate fabrics and wool by dabbing the stain with eucalyptus oil before washing. Launder other fabrics on a very hot wash.

Ice cream: Soak in biological detergent and launder at the highest temperature the fabric will tolerate.

Ink: Dried ink stains are difficult to remove, so soak the garment in cold water. Bleach will restore whites. Launder as usual after soaking.

Ironmould: Cover the stain with lemon juice and fine salt. Leave for an hour, rinse and then launder.

Mildew: Soak white natural fabrics in a bleach solution. On coloured items, dampen the mark, then rub with a block of soap. Leave to dry in a warm place and then launder.

Milk: Rinse in warm water, soak in a biological detergent, and then launder as usual.

Paint:

Acrylic Remove excess with a paper towel, then wash in warm soapy water.

Emulsion Rinse in cold water and then wash as usual.

Gloss Scrape off excess, then dab with white spirit, before washing.

Poster Soak in cold water and then launder as usual.

Perfume: Rinse immediately, then launder. Treat dried stains with equal parts glycerine and water before laundering.

Perspiration: Sponge with ammonia solution of 5 ml to 500 ml (1 teaspoon to 1 pint) water. Rinse immediately and soak in biological detergent, before washing as usual.

Rust: Cover the stain with lemon juice and fine salt. Leave for an hour, rinse and then launder.

Sauces: Rinse in cold running water, then soak in biological detergent before laundering.

Shoe polish: Dab with white spirit before laundering.

Tar: Place folded paper towel over the mark and then dab from below with eucalyptus oil. Launder.

Tea: Rinse in warm water and then soak in biological detergent. Dried stains can be lifted with a glycerine solution.

Wine: Rinse in warm water and then soak in biological detergent before washing as usual.

TRY TO DEVELOP THE HABIT OF WASHING WHITE FABRICS SEPARATELY FROM COLOUREDS TO ENSURE THEY RETAIN THEIR BRIGHT WHITENESS. OCCASIONAL USE OF A LAUNDRY WHITENER WILL ALSO HELP TO KEEP YOUR WHITES LOOKING GOOD.

Hand Washing

These days we all do as little hand washing as possible. Many garment manufacturers make a point of ensuring that their garments, even woollens, are machine-washable, and washing machine companies produce machines with 'delicates' programmes and a slow spin cycle to allow us to machine wash the vast majority of our clothes. However, there are still a few garments that do not respond well to machine washing, or will remain in good condition longer if washed by hand. Good quality underwear, particularly bras, will retain their shape and elasticity longer if hand washed and woollens, especially angora, mohair or cashmere, must all be hand washed in cool water. Tights and stockings are best hand washed, or if machine washed should be enclosed in a net bag to prevent them getting tangled up in the other washing. Certain fabrics such as chiffon, lace and silks and wools also need to be hand washed. Always check the care label in a garment and follow the instructions.

The Technicalities

In general, garments that benefit from hand washing do not benefit from soaking. Hand washing does not mean filling a bowl with soapy water, immersing the garment and going away for an hour. To hand wash successfully, use a gentle detergent such as pure soap flakes or a proprietary liquid soap specifically for hand washing. Add this to a bowl of warm water and immerse the garment, gently squeezing it so that the soapy water penetrates the fibres and lifts any dirt.

Carefully lift the garment out of the bowl of water and refill the bowl with warm water. Rinse thoroughly, repeating the process until no further soap residue is evident. Gently squeeze out the excess moisture. Lightweight fabrics such as silks, chiffon and lace can be hung up to drip dry. Woollens should be laid flat between two clean, dry towels to remove most of the moisture, before being left to dry on a towel-covered flat surface or a jumper drying rack.

FADED BLACK

The fading of black clothes can be caused by a build-up of soap-powder. Colour can sometimes be restored by soaking the garment in warm water to which a little vinegar has been added.

A BUTLER'S SINK IS IDEAL FOR HAND-WASHING GARMENTS. IF YOUR SINK IS TOO SMALL, YOU MAY FIND THAT THE BATH IS A GOOD ALTERNATIVE.

Ironing

Successful ironing is about doing as little of it as possible without one's appearance suffering noticeably. The first step towards this is to fix a hanging rail above the washing machine and tumble dryer. Have this rail well stocked with coat hangers. Garments that cannot be tumble-dried can be given a good shake and then hung on the rail. Those that can be tumble-dried are hung up after drying to allow any residual creases to drop out. Treat your laundry in this way and you will only need to iron pure cotton and linen garments, and nowadays even these fabrics frequently have an easy-care finish, which means that they too need never find their way into the ironing basket.

Line-dried washing does smell wonderfully fresh, but it also tends to be stiffer and more creased. To reduce the need for ironing put the garments in the tumble drier for 10 minutes and then hang them on the rail. They will then be softer and less creased.

Ideally, your ironing board and iron should be left ready for use at all times. In reality, few of us have the space for this, but it is a good idea to ensure that they are easily accessible rather than stuck behind the vacuum cleaner at the back of the hall cupboard. Replace the cover on the board as soon as it shows signs of wear – a heat-reflective surface will make ironing easier. The iron should also be in good condition with un-frayed flex and a clean base. Marks can be removed by rubbing the (cold) base gently with very fine steel wool, taking care not to damage the surface. Follow the manufacturer's instructions on the type of water to use in steam irons and de-scale regularly in hard water areas.

HOW TO IRON

Garments iron most easily when slightly damp. If they are very dry, use a steam iron or spray with water before you start ironing. When ironing a shirt, do the double layers of fabric first – collar, cuffs and around the buttons and buttonholes – then the shoulders and sleeves, and finally the main body of the shirt. Hang it up immediately with the top button fastened. When pressing woven and knitted wool garments, always use a damp cloth to protect the surface of the fabric from damage.

AGA IRONING

If you have an Aga you can use the lids to 'iron' small flat items such as pillowcases, tea towels and napkins. Simply fold them and place them on the lids while still damp. Leave for 15 minutes and then turn them over for another 15 minutes. Hey presto – the ironing is done!

IRONING IS MUCH EASIER
WITH GOOD EQUIPMENT —
USE AN ADJUSTABLE
IRONING BOARD THAT
ALLOWS YOU TO WORK AT
A COMFORTABLE HEIGHT, A
WELL-FITTING COVER AND
AN EFFICIENT IRON.

The Linen Cupboard

Pictures of perfectly pressed and folded linen, neatly tied with ribbon, can leave one feeling somewhat inadequate when confronted with the reality of the average airing cupboard with its jumble of unmatched bed linen, odd socks and towels. The problem with most airing cupboards is that everything goes in it, but little is removed until the occasion when it is next needed. This results in very well aired and frequently very crumpled linen. Where space is at a premium it makes sense to store bed linen, after a brief airing, in the room where it is used. A drawer or cupboard shelf can be allocated for this purpose. Changing beds becomes so much easier when you do away with the need to search the airing cupboard for the right sheet, unfolding half a dozen in your search, and shoving them back less-than-perfectly re-folded as you lose patience.

Where there is space to store all your linen together, good organization will pay dividends, especially if you favour white sheets in a variety of sizes. One of the easiest ways to mark linen is to colour code it with a short length of ribbon sewn on to the hem of each sheet in a similar position. Fold the sheets so that the ribbon is visible and you will be able to tell at a glance what size sheet it is, especially if each size is allocated a particular shelf in the linen cupboard.

Ironing bed linen is a major chore, but nowadays manufacturers are making pure cotton bed linen with an easy-care finish and it is definitely worth the investment. But if sleeping between crisp, starched, cotton or linen sheets is your idea of heaven, investigate if there is a local laundry service – it is a small price to pay for a great pleasure. Let the rest of the family sleep in easy-care cotton while you luxuriate in linen. Bought new, linen is outrageously expensive, but bought from an antique dealer who specializes in bed linen it becomes an affordable luxury.

Lavender Bags and Bottles

'Let's go to that house, for the linen looks white and smells of lavender, and I long to lie in a pair of sheets that smell so.' The Compleat Angler, Izaak Walton (1653).

It is undoubtedly true that sweetly scented linen is a particular and enduring pleasure, as the quote from Izaak Walton illustrates. Three hundred and fifty years later, we still associate the scent of lavender with clean, crisp bed linen. Even if your linen cupboard lacks order, when scented with lavender bags or bottles its contents will give off a fragrance associated with careful housekeeping.

Lavender Bags

The simplest lavender bag need consist of nothing more than a cloth bag filled with dried lavender flowers, but to ensure a long-lasting fragrance the addition of orris root powder and lavender oil is recommended. The orris root powder acts as a fixative for the fragrance, ensuring that the scent endures, but because it is very fine, the bags should be made from a tightly woven cloth, such as a glazed chintz, or a double layer of cotton lawn.

100 g (4 oz) lavender
25 g (1 oz) orris root powder (see suppliers' list)
25 drops lavender oil
4 bags measuring approximately 10 x 15 cm (4 x 6 in)
4 x 20 cm (8 in) lengths of ribbon

Mix together the lavender, orris root and lavender oil in a large bowl. Fill the bags with equal quantities of the mixture and tie the ribbons around the necks of the bags.

Lavender 'Bottles'

This is a traditional way of preserving lavender, with the stems forming a cage around the flowers, allowing the fragrance to be released while keeping the flower heads intact.

For each 'bottle':
25 fresh lavender stems
green garden twine
scissors

Gather the lavender stems into a bundle ensuring that the bases of the flower heads are level with one another. Bind together firmly, but not too tightly, just below the flower heads. Cut off the loose ends of the twine.

Hold the flower heads in one hand and using the other hand, systematically pull the stems over the flower heads until they are fully enclosed by the stems and the 'bottle' has been formed. Bind the stems together about half-way down their length. Use the scissors to trim the ends of the stems level.

BELOW LEFT: Simple lavender 'bottles' can be made more decorative by weaving ribbon between the stems.

BELOW: A lavender wreath is too pretty to conceal inside a linen cupboard. Hang it on the bedroom wall as a fragrant decoration.

RIGHT: A bundle of lavender hung from the handle of an armoir will release its fragrance as the door is opened and closed.

Suppliers' List

Suppliers' List

Pages 12-13
CARPETS AND RUGS
The British Carpet Manufacturers' Association
P.O. Box 1155
New Road
Kidderminster
Worcs DY10 1WW
Tel: 01562 747351
Basic information and leaflets on all types of carpeting; if they are unable to help they will refer you on for more technical help

Pages 14-15
SISAL, RUSH AND COIR MATTING
Natural Carpets Ltd
Talent House
Charlton
Hants SP10 4AX
Tel: 01264 336845

Crucial Trading
The Plaza
535 Kings Road
London SW10 0SZ
Tel: 020 7376 7100
or
79 Westbourne Park Road
London W2 5QH
Tel: 020 7221 9000

Pages 16-17
CURTAINS AND BLINDS
The British Blind & Shutter Association
Heath Street
Tamworth
Staffs B79 7JH
Tel: 01827 52337
Supplies list of contractors who will clean or repair blinds and shutters

Tidmarsh & Sons
32 Hyde Way
Welwyn Garden City
Herts AL7 3AW
Tel: 01707 886226
Good quality blinds made to measure. Mail order available

The Curtain Exchange
Tel: 020 7731 8316 for your nearest branch
Good quality second-hand curtains bought and sold

Pages 18-19
ANTIQUE TEXTILES
The Textile Conservation Centre
Apartment 22
Hampton Court Palace
East Molesey
Surrey KT8 9AU
Tel: 020 8977 4943
Professional conservation of antique textiles

or
Burghley House
Burghley Park
Stamford
Lincs PE9 3JY
Tel: 01780 480188

The Chelsea Brocante Antiques Fair
Chelsea Old Town Hall
Kings Road
London SW3 5EE
Good source of antique textiles

The Decorative Antiques & Textiles Fair
The Marquee
Kings College
Chelsea
London SW3
Good source of antique textiles

The Kensington Brocante Antiques Fair
Kensington Town Hall
Hornton Street
London W8 7NX
Good source of antique textiles

Sarah Meysey-Thompson Antiques
10 Church Street
Woodbridge
Suffolk IP12 1DH
Tel: 01394 382144
Good source of antique textiles

Pages 20-23
WOODEN FURNITURE AND FLOORS
The Hardwood Flooring Company
146 West End Lane
London NW6 1SD
Tel: 0171 328 8481

Woodhouse
Unit 6
Quarry Farm Industrial Estate
Staplecross Road
Bodiam
East Sussex TN32 5RA
Tel: 01580 831700

British Wood Preserving Association
4 Romford Road
London E15 4EA
Tel: 020 8519 2588
Technical advice, leaflets and recommended contractors for wood treatment

Picreator Enterprises Ltd
44 Park View Gardens
Hendon
London NW4 2PN
Tel: 020 8202 8972
Renaissance Wax

J W Bollom & Co Ltd
Croydon Road
Elmers End
Beckenham
Kent BR3 4BL
Tel: 020 8658 2299
*Briwax floor polish. Ring for the
address of your local retailer*

Pages 24-25
Silver, Brass and Bronze
*Renaissance Wax (see previous
listing) – protective wax coating
for metalware*

National Trust Enterprises
Western Way
Melksham
Wilts SN12 8DZ
Tel: 01225 704545
Plate brushes for cleaning silver

Pages 30-33
FIREPLACES AND STOVES
**National Association of
Chimney Sweeps**
St Mary's Chambers
19 Station Road
Stone
Staffs ST15 8JP
Tel: 01785 811732
*Will help you find a local
chimney sweep*

**The National Fireplace
Association**
P O Box 1200
Freepost BN2043
Birmingham B11 2BD
Tel: 0121 200 1310
*General information on fireplaces
and fuels*

The Solid Fuel Association
7 Swanwick Court
Alfreton
Derbyshire DE55 7AS
*Advice on types and uses of
solid fuel*

A Bell & Co
Kingsthorpe Works
Kingsthorpe Road
Northampton NN2 6LT
Tel: 01604 712505
*Suppliers of specialist cleaning
materials for marble and stone*

*Renaissance Wax (see previous
listing) – protective surface for
marble*

Pages 34-37
POTPOURRIS
The Hop Shop
Castle Farm
Shoreham
Sevenoaks
Kent TN14 7UB
Tel: 01959 523219
*Ingredients for potpourri. Mail
order service*

Hambleden Herbs
Court Farm
Milverton
Somerset TA4 1NF
Tel: 01823 401001
Ingredients for potpourri

Pages 42-45
THE BED
The Sleep Council
High Corn Mill
Chapel Hill
Skipton
N Yorks BD23 1NL
Advice on buying beds

The Odd Mattress Factory
Cumeragh House
Cumeragh Lane
Whittingham
Preston
Lancs PR3 2AL
Tel: 01772 786666
*Handmade mattresses to fit non-
standard sizes of bed*

**The Decorative Antiques &
Textiles Fair**
The Marquee
Kings College
Chelsea
London SW3
Antique bed linen

John Lewis Partnership
Tel: 020 7629 7711 for nearest
branch
Contemporary bed linen

Monogrammed Linen Shop
168 & 184 Walton Street
London SW3 2JL
Tel: 020 7589 4033

The White Company
298-300 Munster Road
London SW6 6BH
Tel: 020 7385 7988
Mail order linen

Toast
Llanfynydd
Carmarthenshire SA32 7TT
Tel: 01558 668800
Mail order linen

Pages 46-49
CLOTHES
The Holding Company
241-245 Kings Road
London SW3 5EL
and
41 Spring Gardens
Manchester M2 2BG
Tel: 0161 8343400
Original storage solutions.
Tel: 020 7610 9160 for mail
order nationwide

Hambleden Herbs (see
previous listing) – *tonquin beans
and orris root powder for moth-
repellent sachets*

Culpeper Ltd
Hadstock Road
Linton
Cambridge CB1 6NJ
Tel: 01223 891196
*Tonquin beans and orris root
powder for moth-repellent sachets*

Pages 50-51
POMANDERS
Hambleden Herbs (see
previous listing) – *ingredients
and essential oils*

Neal's Yard Remedies
29 John Dalton Street
Manchester M2 6DS
Tel: 0161 831 7875
*Ingredients and essential oils.
Mail order available*

Pages 52-55
CREAMS, LOTIONS AND COSMETICS
Hambleden Herbs (see
previous listing) – *rose water,
white beeswax and essential oils*

G. Baldwin & Co
173 Walworth Road
London SE17 1RW
Tel: 020 7703 5550
Rose water and white beeswax

Pages 56-57
HAIR CARE
Hambleden Herbs (see
previous listing) – *dried herbs*

Culpeper Ltd (see previous
listing) – *dried herbs*

Pages 60-61
BATHROOM CLEANING
Bath Doctor
34 London Road
Faversham
Kent ME13 8RX
Tel: 01795 591711
Renovation of old enamel baths

Tile Promotion Board
Forum Court
83 Copers Cope Road
Beckenham
Kent BR3 1NR
Tel: 020 8663 1569
*Leaflet on choosing and caring
for tiles*

Lakeland Ltd
Alexandra Buildings
Windermere
Cumbria LA23 1BQ
Cleaning products
Tel: 015394 88100 for mail
order; tel: 015394 88200 for
information on your nearest
shop

Pages 62-65
FIRST AID AND NATURAL REMEDIES
Hambleden Herbs (see
previous listing) – *medicinal and
culinary herbs*

Neal's Yard Remedies (see
previous listing) – *medicinal and
culinary herbs*

Culpeper Ltd (see previous
listing) – *medicinal and culinary
herbs*

Pages 70-71
CHINA
Good Housekeeping Institute
National Magazine House
72 Broadwick Street
London W1V 2BP
*Fact sheet (price £2) giving
details of china manufacturers
offering a china matching service*

Pages 74-75
CUTLERY
The Tarnprufe Company Ltd
68 Nether Edge Road
Sheffield S7 1RX
Tel: 0114 2553 652
Tarnish-proof cutlery bags

Pages 76-77
KITCHEN FLOORS
Keswick Flooring
Heron House
Riverside Farm, Low Road
Forncett St. Mary
Norfolk NR16 1JJ
Tel: 0800 592 739
Suppliers of all types of flooring

Fired Earth
Twyford Mill
Oxford Road
Adderbury
Oxfordshire OX17 3HP
Tel: 01295 812088
Tile and stone flooring

Forbo-Nairn
P O Box 1
Kirkcaldy
Fife KY1 2SB
Tel: 01592 643111
Linoleum and Marmoleum

Wicander
Amorium House
Star Road
Partridge Green
Horsham
West Sussex RH13 8RA
Tel: 01403 710002
Cork flooring

Pages 78-81
PAINTWORK
Auro Organic Paints
White Horse House
Ashdon
Nr. Saffron Waldon
Essex CB10 2ET
Tel: 01799 584888
*Mail order organic paints,
pigments and varnishes*

Biofa Natural Paints
5 School Road
Kidlington
Oxford OX5 2HB
Tel: 01867 54964
*Naturally and environmentally
safe paints, pigments and
varnishes*

Farrow & Ball
33 Uddens Trading Estate
Wimbourne
Dorset BH21 7NL
National Trust Historic paints.
Tel: 01202 876141 for colour
card and stockists

Papers & Paints
4 Park Walk
London SW10 0AD
Tel: 020 7352 8626
Paint matching service

WINDOWS

Pages 82-83

**The Glass & Glazing
Federation**
44-48 Borough High Street
London SE1 1XB
Tel: 020 7403 7177
Advice on cleaning all glass

Pages 82-97
Good Housekeeping Institute
Tel: 09067 529080
Advice on food and cookery

Pages 96-97
HERBS AND SPICES
Hambleden Herbs (see
previous listing) – *organic
culinary herbs and spices*

Culpeper Ltd (see previous
listing) – *dried herbs and spices*

Fox's Spices Ltd
Mason's Road Industrial Estate
Stratford upon Avon
Warwickshire CV37 9NF
Tel: 01789 266420
Herbs and spices

Iden Croft Herbs
Frittenden Road
Staplehurst
Kent TN12 0DH
Tel: 01580 891432
Herb plants

Pages 102-103
DEALING WITH PESTS
*Your local council will have a pest
control officer or a list of local
companies.*

Rentokil
Tel: 01342 833022 for your
local branch

Pages 104-105
PETCARE
RSPCA
Causeway
Horsham
West Sussex RH12 1HG
HYPERLINK
http://www.rspca.org.uk for
petcare info
Tel: 0870 555999 to report an
animal in distress

Pages 108-111
STAIN REMOVAL
Lakeland Ltd (see previous
listing) – Dye Magnet

**The Beckmann Stain
Advisory Service**
(manufacturers of Stain Devils)
Dendron Ltd
Watford
Herts WD1 7JJ
Advice on stain removal

Pages 120-121
LAVENDER BAGS AND BOTTLES
Norfolk Lavender
Caley Mill
Heacham
King's Lynn
Norfolk PE31 7JE
Tel: 01485 570384
*Dried lavender and lavender oil
by mail order*

OTHER USEFUL ADDRESSES
Country Living by Post
P O Box 81
Shaftesbury
Dorset SP7 8TA
Tel: 01747 854092
*Catalogue and Country Living
paint range*

The Victorian Society
1 Priory Gardens
London W4 1TT
Tel: 020 8994 1019
*Booklets for sale on caring for
houses of the period on subjects
such as fireplaces, doors and
paintwork*

The Building Centre
26 Store Street
London WC1E 7BT
Tel: 020 7637 1022
*Useful advice, sample materials
and fittings if you are undertaking
building work*

**The Conservation Unit
Museum & Galleries
Commission**
16 Queen Anne's Gate
London SW1H 9AA
Tel: 020 7233 3683
*Conservation workshops and
useful leaflets*

English Heritage
Fortress House
3 Savile Row
London W1X 2HE
Tel: 020 797 33000
*Advice on permitted work on
listed houses*

The Georgian Group
37 Spital Square
London E1 6DY
Tel: 020 7739 6563
*Authoritative information on all
aspects of Georgian architecture
and interiors*

ARCHITECTURAL
RECLAMATION YARDS
**LASSCO
London Architectural Salvage
Company**
Mark Street (off Paul Street)
London EC2A 4ER
Tel: 020 7739 0448

Walcot Reclamation
The Depot
Riverside Business Park
Lower Bristol Road
Bath BA2 3DW
Tel: 01225 335532

SALVO
Ford Woodhouse
Berwick on Tweed
Northumberland TD15 2QF
Tel: 01668 216494
*Architectural reclamation listings
magazine*

Index

picture acknowledgments

Caroline Arber: pages 7, 26 (top), 44, 72, 101,
    105, 109, 113, 117
Jan Baldwin: pages 50, 92, 94
Tim Beddow: pages 22, 28
Clive Boursnell: page 85
Yvonne Catterson: page 51
Charlie Colmer: pages 37, 61
Harry Cory Wright: pages 36, 73, 81
Christopher Drake: pages 2, 5, 10, 14, 15, 18, 19,
    30, 31, 45, 53, 66, 70, 78
Andreas von Einsiedel: pages 8, 17, 119
Kate Gadsby: pages 39 (right), 77
David George: page 29
Melvin Grey: page 16 (left)
Huntley Hedworth: pages 38, 39 (left), 68, 71, 118
Frank Herholdt: page 27
Christopher Hill: pages 69, 83
Tom Leighton: page 114
Lisa Linder: pages 48 (left and right), 49
Simon McBride: page 58
Jill Mead: pages 34, 50, 56, 57
James Merrell: pages 16 (right), 24 (right), 43, 47,
    74, 75, 98, 106
Gloria Nicol: pages 120 (left and right), 121
Debbie Patterson: page 63
Bridget Peirson: pages 62, 64, 65 (top and bottom),
    96 (left and right), 97
Alex Ramsey: pages 21, 23, 33
Trevor Richards: page 90
Kim Sayer: page 55
Pia Tryde: pages 13, 24 (left), 25, 76, 78, 104, 110
Simon Upton: page 40
Peter Williams: pages 1, 89
Ling Wong: page 86
Polly Wreford: page 26 (bottom)

Styling by Hester Page, Ben Kendrick,
Pippa Rimmer, Kathy Ward, Nicola Goodwin,
Karen McCartney, Katrin Cargill, Gabi Tubbs.